INTEGRATING NEWLY
MERGED ORGANIZATIONS

INTEGRATING NEWLY MERGED
ORGANIZATIONS

MICHAEL P. GENDRON

Westport, Connecticut
London

Library of Congress Cataloging-in-Publication Data

Gendron, Michael.
    Integrating newly merged organizations / Michael P. Gendron.
        p.   cm.
    Includes bibliographical references and index.
    ISBN 0–56720–316–7 (alk. paper)
    1. Consolidation and merger of corporations—Management.   2. Consolidation
and merger of corporations—Planning.   3. Organizational behavior.
4. Personnel management.   I. Title.
HD58.8.G46 2004
658.1'62—dc22   2003062437

British Library Cataloguing in Publication Data is available.

Library of Congress Catalog Card Number: 2003062437
ISBN: 1–56720–316–7

First published in 2004

Praeger Publishers, 88 Post Road West, Westport, CT 06881
An imprint of Greenwood Publishing Group, Inc.
www.praeger.com

Printed in the United States of America

∞™

The paper used in this book complies with the
Permanent Paper Standard issued by the National
Information Standards Organization (Z39.48–1984).

10 9 8 7 6 5 4 3 2 1

Contents

Exhibits

Preface

Throughout my career, I have concentrated on delivering value to the stockholders by applying my training in areas such as accounting, planning and strategy, treasury, and international operations. I've worked all over the world in many industries, ranging from short-cycle consumer and high-technology businesses, to the slower paced capital goods industry, to service industries. Early in my career, my contribution was limited to *doing* as an individual contributor. As I matured in both personal and business experience, I eventually led the finance, administration, and information technology functions, and I became the CFO of companies, ranging from one of the "Hottest Growth Companies in America" to a billion-dollar global company. This mosaic of experience and training was the basis of my drive to increase value through M&A business integration by planning and executing—and not just *strategizing*.

Early in my career, it seemed that many M&A activities and strategies that companies embarked upon just didn't happen in the *real world*. Although the *theoretical numbers* proved beyond any doubt that *it*—the company acquisition, the newly acquired product, the new distributor venture, and so forth—would add value, *it* often didn't happen as expected. *The Wall Street Journal, Business Week, Fortune, Forbes,* and other publications often boldly reported these failures. In fact, perhaps more than 60 percent of the time, acquisitions don't add value.

While at Bausch & Lomb in the 1980s, I learned that developing a well-thought-out plan focusing on the critical success factors that support the numbers and executing the plan completely were necessary to make *it* happen. Also, while executing plans, I noticed that *stuff*—a technical term used in business that applies to almost anything—often changed quite unpredictably, which required modifying the plan. I discovered *stuff*—things that changed without notice—by observing activity, talking with the people involved, and asking the questions, "Is everything going according to plan? What else should we do to make *it* happen?" And then I listened to the responses. If an issue required resolution, I ensured that decisions were made, and then I communicated the decision to the right people. Seems simple enough.

This book is designed to help the executive develop effective integration plans, identify *stuff,* and successfully integrate acquisitions. Just before I wrote this book, I read all the books I could find describing the *issues* and the possible *solutions* in M&A execution, integration, and deal making; I found that none of them approached the task as I envisioned in this book. I wrote *Integrating Newly Merged Organizations,* put the manuscript in my office for a year or so, rewrote the book to better reflect my thoughts about the process, and sent the manuscript to the publisher.

"C" level executives who decide that mergers and acquisitions represent a wonderful opportunity for profitable growth and stock appreciation and also understand that such expansion is a risky venture should read this book. Ideally these executives will read the book and share it with members of their organization, suggesting that the issues covered in the book should be included in the planning and execution of future acquisitions. I hope that these execs find *Integrating Newly Merged Organizations* to be a comprehensive, practical book that gives some specific guidelines to improve the success rate of their M&A program.

ACKNOWLEDGMENTS

I couldn't have written this book without the experience that several executives encouraged me to get—and allowed me to enjoy. Many thanks to Mike Buettner, Diane Harris, Steve Kelbley, John Loughlinm, and especially Jim Ward—at the time, executives with Bausch & Lomb Inc. During my developmental years, these executives introduced me to the M&A challenges. With their guidance and support, I worked through many acquisitions and divestitures in many industries and countries, learning the technical requirements and the art of the successful M&A transaction. This book is a compilation of the strategies, techniques, processes, and art that I've used over the years and observations that I've made during the challenging and hectic M&A transactions I've managed.

Acquisition Integration: A Critical Task

THE ACQUISITION

A business acquisition may represent the single largest investment that your company will ever make. An acquisition becomes even more significant when you consider that you may not just be risking the out-of-pocket investment in another company, but you also may actually be risking the very existence of your established operation. Business combinations are indeed very risky: "Most studies show that 60%–70% of takeovers do not pay off, at least when gauged by the share price of the dealmakers vs. their peers or market benchmarks."[1] When challenged, CEOs will often admit that the acquisitions did not meet established internal criteria. But companies continue to merge, challenge the odds, and take enormous business risk. See Exhibit 1.1 for examples of some unsuccessful mergers.

It need not be so risky, however, as several well-accomplished companies have routinely demonstrated. Companies such as Cisco, General Electric, and Citigroup have routinely acquired companies within their existing product lines, new venture companies, small and large companies, and companies in new geographies, and they have done so very successfully. This does not mean that every combination is a thriving success, but rather that they have an established process that allows them to generally meet their merger objectives.

An acquisition and integration project blends different cultures, organizations, and policies into a single, functional unit in a very compressed

EXHIBIT 1.1 Some Unsuccessful Mergers

Year	Company	Goal	Results
1996	Union Pacific and Southern Pacific	The $4 billion deal was to have created a "seamless" rail network from the Midwest to the West Coast.	The reality was complete gridlock.
1997	HFS and CUC International	This $14 billion deal to create Cendant was intended to build a marketing powerhouse.	But accounting irregularities at CUC sent Cendant's share price down 46 percent in one day and triggered a federal probe.
1998	Conseco and Green Tree Financial	With the $7.6 billion acquisition of lender Green Tree, insurer Conseco foresaw a bonanza.	But Green Tree was hit by huge charges on bad loans.
1998	Daimler-Benz and Chrysler	Daimler paid $36 billion for Chrysler, then the hottest U.S. auto maker.	But huge losses, botched product introductions, spiraling costs, and a demoralized U.S. workforce have wiped out $60 billion in market value.
1999	Aetna and Prudential Healthcare	Aetna hoped that the $1 billion deal would make it the number one HMO.	But Prudential and a string of troubled mergers led to the ouster of Aetna's CEO. Now, the company is breaking in two.
1999	AlliedSignal and Honeywell	AlliedSignal hoped to combine its efficiency with Honeywell's product innovation.	Instead, the $14 billion combo got hit by rising oil prices, a plunging Euro, and management problems.
1999	AT&T/TCI/Mediaone	AT&T's back-to-back deals for TCI and Mediaone, for a combined $90 billion, backfired on CEO C. Michael Armstrong. He tried to sell consumers on packaged telecom services, but AT&T's core businesses dried up.	Now, with its shares in the tank, AT&T is breaking up again.
1999	Federated Department stores and Fingerhut	Federated paid $1.7 billion to apply Fingerhut's direct-marketing skills to its Macy's and Bloomingdale's units.	But Fingerhut's focus on low-end consumers led to huge write-offs.
1999	Mattel and Learning Co.	Mattel hoped to break into the CD-ROM game market with the $3.5 billion purchase.	But then the Internet caught on, drying up the CD-ROM market. Mattel's stock crashed, and CEO Jill Barad was ousted.
1999	McKesson and HBO	The $12 billion merger of the number one drug wholesaler McKesson and medical software maker HBO & Co. ran into a buzz saw.	Auditors uncovered an accounting scandal at HBO, leading to resignations and criminal charges. McKesson shares are off 47 percent for the year.

Source: "Let's Talk Turkey," *Business Week*, December 11, 2000, 44.

timeframe. Strong leadership and teamwork among personnel at both companies are critical, or the acquisition will fail to meet established goals. Good planning, tight accountability, and excellent communication are essential for success.

An acquisition and merger is definitely complex. Exhibit 1.2, however, does not display all the activities and planning considerations necessary to fully understand what is necessary for a successful integration. That is one reason why well-trained personnel—ideally from the due diligence team—who are fully dedicated to the merger and well informed about the strategy and business goals are critical elements of the integration process.

THE RISKS

Exhibit 1.2 displays some of the elements that make business combinations very risky. The graphic can be duplicated for every location, department, and work group in both companies. People, facilities, organizations, established processes, product lines, customer contracts, and so on vary from company to company. Making change is difficult. All of the tangible variables, and intangible ones such as personalities, informal processes, and business relationships, may be shattered by the business combinations.

EXHIBIT 1.2   Business Integration Complexities

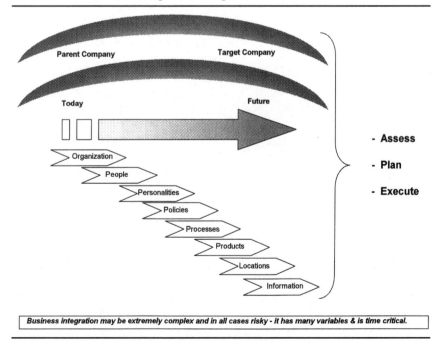

Business integration may be extremely complex and in all cases risky - it has many variables & is time critical.

As this book examines each of these individual variables, it becomes clear that each has an entirely new subset of variables.

Consider people as a simple variable. Initially, a company may appear to be the sum of 2,000 employees. In any thorough analysis, however, the reviewer will try to segment these into meaningful groups to better understand the factors that motivate the people, assess the impact of the merger on the selected groups, plan an integration process, and finally execute the plan for the desired objective. (See Exhibit 1.3.)

Let's examine some of the components. Engineers, accountants, and hourly employees will have their own personal impressions of the merger regardless of the commitments made by company management. Selected functions—engineers, accountants, hourly employees, and so on—at *each company* may have different impressions of the merger regardless of these commitments. Moreover, the same functions—for example, accountants at the headquarters, the manufacturing plants, the sales branches, and the distribution centers—each may have different impressions of the merger regardless of these commitments. These potentially different interpretations or levels of trust create risk, and the risk is not just limited to the company acquired. If you don't manage the integration properly, you may also be risking the financial health of the base business. If you lose control of the integration, you may lose control of the entire investment in both companies.

THE COSTS

The cost of an acquisition may exceed the out-of-pocket cost incurred to buy the company or the assets of an organization. Each incremental activity related to the merger would take valuable resource from serving the customers—the fundamental activity that makes employees and stockholders happy and profitable. Carly Fiorina, CEO of Hewlett-Packard, has stated that more than a million man-hours have been spent on the planning/integration process of the Hewlett-Packard and Compaq merger,[2] and that is early in the process. (See Exhibit 1.4.)

During any integration, there are lapses in focus due to personal concerns by employees, confusion about next steps, poor coordination, or communications breakdowns. Inefficiencies are also one of the key costs. Keith Symmers of Best Practices LLC has stated, "Productivity can fall by as much as 50% while employees are in limbo awaiting new assignments."[3] Tabulate 40–50 percent of the total cost of running your operation and add that as the inefficiency costs of running the target company to understand the real total cost. In other words, if employee costs total $5 million per month, inefficiency can total $2.5 million per month.

Time will be a major consideration in any merger. If the integration process is not planned and executed extremely well, delays and additional

EXHIBIT 1.3 Two Companies to Merge

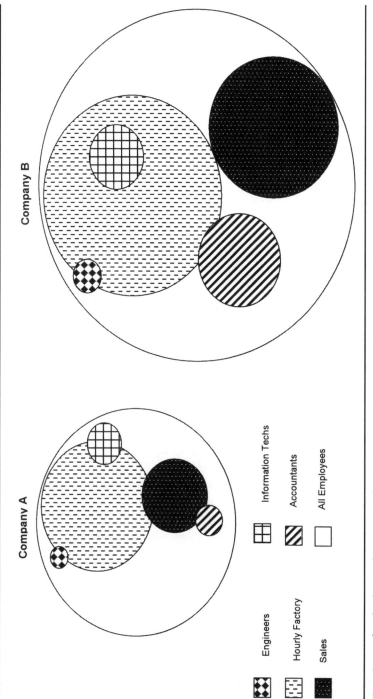

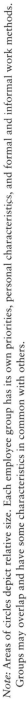

Note: Areas of circles depict relative size. Each employee group has its own priorities, personal characteristics, and formal and informal work methods. Groups may overlap and have some characteristics in common with others.

EXHIBIT 1.4   Integration Is Time Critical

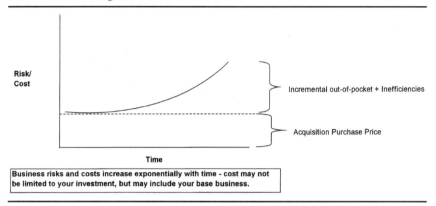

Risk/Cost

Time

Incremental out-of-pocket + Inefficiencies

Acquisition Purchase Price

Business risks and costs increase exponentially with time - cost may not be limited to your investment, but may include your base business.

cost will result. Delays may also impact the morale of the employees (in both companies) and adversely impact your customers' confidence. The Hewlett-Packard and Compaq merger is perhaps one of the largest tech mergers in U.S. history. The executives at each company know the value and risks of the merger, and have invested "months and millions of hours of integration planning by [their] teams"[4] to make sure the merger was completed smoothly. On May 7, 2002, three days after Compaq was acquired, Hewlett-Packard announced the basic company structure and key leadership positions.

WHAT TO DO?

Because most business combinations fail to meet the objectives, but some companies do extremely well at the integration process, there must be a process or formula that allows them to succeed. This book will describe some of the actions that companies routinely take to make an acquisition successful. Throughout the book, several common themes will be discussed:

- Understand the current situation—the "as is" state of each business.
- Understand the "to be" state of the combined business—what the combined business will look like in the future.
- There is a critical link between success in the integration process and a well-prepared due diligence review, and both aspects should have common team members. Use the best people in every functional area to make the merger a success (remember the cost of delay and failure?).
- Effective communication is critical to the success of any business combination.
- Take care of the people; understand the company cultures. Be honest and forth-right in all communications, and deal with the "people" issues as they arise.
- Each business is unique, but using "master templates" of each business process will minimize missed opportunities.

Although there is no single, all-inclusive master plan that can be applied to every merger, the goal of the book is to acquaint the reader with some basic activities that should be considered by business executives and functional experts in the people, communications, and business processes that are important to a successful integration.

The book includes many different kinds of checklists, or evaluation matrices. These are included to identify some key elements that should be evaluated or considered in an integration process. They are not meant to be strictly followed. It would be very easy to perform the documented steps and entirely miss the judgments required. When you review an exhibit, therefore, consider the key elements and don't focus too heavily on the detail.

The book also frequently refers to functional specialists—for example, human resources, finance, and legal. Quite often in small companies, one individual is responsible for many functional areas, so don't be offended by the structure shown here. Once again, the book's objective is to establish a specific responsibility based on a generic company in which all functional activities must be performed.

This book intentionally leaves the individual functional area reviews until late in the text. The early chapters will focus on the key elements to success. That is, define where you want to be, establish the organization structure, and properly staff the organization to get the job done. There is a section (See Chapter 4) to help identify the constituents: those who will be affected by any integration, including some not ordinarily considered. Those constituents include vendors, local communities, contract employees, agents, and part-time employees. I also spend some time talking about activities that are very important to the employees: payroll, benefits, and performance measurement systems. These activities—taking care of the employees—will lead to a successful integration.

Once you know where you are going and properly assemble the team of experts, the integration task becomes much simpler. When these experts are in place, simply prioritize the issues and let the people do their jobs.

QUICK CHECK OF CHAPTER 1

✓ High risk; high failure rate

✓ People driven

✓ High cost

✓ Time critical

2

Why Buy the Company?

This chapter will explore why acquisitions are made—the true reasons may not simply be more sales or near-term earnings. Are there key processes being acquired as the basis of a valuation? Are there critical employees? Are there new geographies being captured? While many factors may result with higher near-term sales, the strategic reason must be properly understood to protect the critical elements of the acquisition. As a company is reviewed, the management team should focus on the "optimum new company." Think of the company in a future state—a "to be" state—and do not think about two separate companies or simply a combined company. A successfully reconfigured company is based on the best process, the best people, and the best organization based on the combined company strategy.

The due diligence/integration team should approach the analysis from an unbiased point of view, not as a component of either company, and it should focus on the optimum company that is potentially as large as the combined operation, with the right organization size and composition. After the successful conclusion of the acquisition process, the company may be substantially different from either of the original companies.

The acquisition team should define the purpose of the acquisition, either within the formal strategic planning process or informally, before any initial negotiations to either acquire a company or establish a joint venture. This is a critical step since the due diligence review, the negotiation, and the integration (if required) will be driven by the purpose. Consider the impact of an acquisition completed primarily to acquire geographic cover-age—for example, European presence in a regulated market. If geography is the driving force behind the acquisition, the company should thoroughly understand the implications of territory expansion through thorough investigation. Fundamental parts of each business such as their reporting relationships, functional control, or cultures may affect both the acquiring company and the target company. Due diligence should concentrate on the important geographic issues. Integration or assimilation plans should begin in the conceptual deal structure and pricing model, and should be reviewed and confirmed in the due diligence review by identifying important risks/opportunities within the geography expansion strategy. Factors such as legal integration, statutory filings, distributor and subsidiary relation-ships, as well as key personnel could impact the deal.

There are several ways to define the strategic intent or best fit of an acquisition. Examples of strategic intent can include:

Market expansion. This could include existing products or new products in the development pipeline, customers, or geographic growth. Market expansion would also include established relationships, patents, or licenses. In the 1990s Compaq Computer acquired Tandem Computers (expanded product lines to fault-tolerant computers) as well as Digital Equipment (new chip sets, the mini-computer market segment, and a highly qualified service organization). Products or licenses within the development pipeline and in-process customer and geo-graphic relationships may not be visible to a third party and should be a factor in the due diligence review.

Process. The target company may have unique or extraordinary processes that help to achieve the strategic goals of the acquiring company. One consideration in the Daimler-Benz acquisition of Chrysler (in addition to the U.S. market share) was the rapid design process and desirable styling capabilities of Chrysler. If process is the key to the acquisition, these processes should be evaluated and investigated dur-ing the due diligence/integration process, then reviewed to determine the best method to protect that value and effectively integrate the processes after the acquisition.

People. Experts in a particular field may be the primary reason for an acquisi-tion. During the late 1990s, technical experts developed overnight in new tech-nologies within the medical, biotech, software and computer hardware, and tele-com industries. These experts often migrate to entrepreneurial firms, which have a more personal character and demand results. This has been a consistent mode of expansion for Cisco in the telecom and routing business. The key in any such integration project is to guard those key people and ensure a smooth transition.

Financial expansions. These are completed to gain economic advantage, for example through economies of scale or diversity of the business cycle. Citibank has acquired CIT Insurance to expand its product lines and to diversify its economic risk.

Although there may be a primary purpose for an acquisition, there may be several additional and important reasons for the acquisition. For example, when Compaq acquired Digital, the acquisition also established a foothold in the minicomputer market segment. This opened new opportunities in small business relationships and in scientific applications in laboratories. As the integration team reviewed the priorities, several of these business advantages could be established as priorities. Some elements, however, may be lost due to prioritization of the "value" of the acquisition to the target company.

Prioritization will help to focus the due diligence review activities, due diligence and integration team selection, and preliminary integration/ disposition steps. It is important to specifically *define and document the purpose of the acquisition* to ensure that a proper review and transition plan are developed and implemented. Exhibit 2.1 reflects an example of specifications for a particular acquisition.

PURPOSE

The specific purpose or strategic intent of the acquisition will determine the type and extent of planning and review required. Although there may be other reasons to acquire a company or organization, this chapter will discuss the purpose of the acquisition by examining four of the primary reasons for acquisitions: process improvement, market, people, and financial priorities. These broad categories should include the purpose of most acquisitions. Once the primary purpose to acquire has been identified and the other major reasons to buy have been prioritized, the "to be" state used in the valuation and integration process can be more easily defined, and the actual integration task becomes less risky. Consider some of the major acquisitions of the 1990s and the apparent gaps in the acquiring business. It is important that there is a stated strategic intent.

The Process

Definition of an "end" state or of a "to be" state is an essential part of defining the purpose. Once a company understands where it will be, it is easier to map or define step by step how it will get there. Process improvement or acquiring new processes may be the primary purpose for many acquisitions. "Process" can include *any process in the value chain or particular subprocesses within functional areas that are unique in the target company.* Several examples of primary functional processes that may be desirable in an acquisition are:

• New product development and R&D
• Sales
• Service

EXHIBIT 2.1   Screening Checklist

Criteria	Key Company Specifications		
	Critical Assessment Factors	Checkpoints	Responsibility
PURPOSE			
Add complementary products with sales of $10 million.	Use common manufacturing and distribution channels		
FINANCIAL			
Minimum **Company** size of $10 million	Company Sales		Business Dev
Compound **Annual Growth** of 10% per year	Historical Growth (3 years) & projected future		
Minimum **Return on Net Assets** of 20% annually	Return on Assets		
Minimum **Sales** per headcount of $300,000	Validate fulltime headcount/sustainability/org chart		
PRODUCT			
Product development cycle of 3 years	Review product pipeline, R&D process; sustainable & transferable; personnel retention critical		R&D
Product will require simple electronic assembly			
Vertical Integration minimal, with subassembly ops.	Vertical integration minimal		Manufacturing
GEOGRAPHIC			
US manufacturer	Northeast preferred; ISO 9000		
Distribution global; concentration in Europe	Validate foreign distributor relationships		Sales
FUNCTIONAL REVIEW			
Primary Functions			
Inbound Logistics	...ease of transfer to parent purchasing		Distribution
Operations	Quality standards must conform; transfer top 5 products to parent 2nd shift		Quality
Outbound Logistics	...decentralized distribution electronically linked to parent company HQ		MIS
Support Functions			
Finance	...transition to parent ERP system		MIS
Legal			
PEOPLE			

Note: It is useful to standardize the vetting checklist for all acquisitions to ensure that subtle components of valuation are not overlooked. The master checklist should have assigned responsibilities so that the evaluation is consistently assessed.

- Manufacturing operations
- Administrative processes

In each of the functions, the process in the target company should be thoroughly analyzed to understand the key elements of process success (i.e., equipment, training, unique materials, and new science), source (i.e., whether driven by culture or specific people), sustainability, and transferability. Sustainability and transferability are important since these assessments will determine the future value of the process to the company. If a successful process cannot be sustained over a reasonable future period (e.g., it is important to know that the source of raw materials, such as stem cells in biotech research, has a useful life of only two years) or reasonably transferred if required, the value of the deal is diminished. A qualitative process assessment will allow the team to understand how the traits can be transferred and/or maintained to a new combined company. While due diligence team members may provide input and an initial assessment, the process should ultimately be assessed by a senior manager to ensure the credibility and accountability of the assessment.

As critical processes are identified, the team should be sure that it considers the sustainability and transferability of the process, which may include people. Have you ever worked in an organization where the key elements to a process were informal, undocumented, and known by only a few people? If these people were to leave, what is the value of the company? Beware: Protect yourself and your company from unforeseen integration problems.

R&D Process

For example, an R&D development group in a small technology-driven company may have a loyal and dedicated core team, and a high turnover in the other highly specialized development staff due to very favorable market conditions. The management group—that loyal, dedicated core team—may be driven by the entrepreneurial culture and as a result will consistently develop new innovative products. The group may rely heavily on informal communications and on adequate but not ISO-quality procedures and documentation. If a company such as GM or AT&T acquired such a company, the valued entrepreneurial spirit may be lost due to extensive required protocols—and the value would be destroyed. In this case, it is critical to guard the spirit of the small company or the R&D process may not be transferable.

Process transferability is dependent upon an organization's willingness to change and adapt. Examine the workforce, understand the process, and look for indicators that drive the process. You may find that the elements of success include factors such as extensive training, open forums/group leadership, and union/nonunion environments. *Process transferability applies to both the acquired and the acquiring company.* Examine your own processes with the same critical eye.

If one selected area is not a priority within the acquisition (e.g., the R&D process), you may want to consider how it would fit with your operations and the extent of effort required for integration. It may be necessary to modify your plans if there is not a good fit except for the isolated target process. If you identify outlying processes that are not managed consistently with your processes, you'll have to develop modification or disposition activities to clean up the acquisition for a complete integration.

Another important example of a process priority is product development cycle times that were important competitive weapons in many highly competitive markets during the 1990s. Cycle time from product development to sale is a part of the value chain that dominated the highly competitive 1990s. Extensive use of CAD systems, interactive graphics, and real-time information sharing through the Internet and intranets have changed the competitive environment. For example, during the 1990s, Boeing had completely designed the new 777 on CAD systems, providing for customer feedback and manufacturing capability assessment, and reducing overall design-to-production time by years and hundreds of millions of dollars. Chrysler now designs and produces a new model in two years compared to four years previously, creating a significant cost savings and market design competitive advantage. Such business development cycles may be worth hundreds of millions of dollars of profits to a competitor operating with outdated technology and processes.

During the 1990s, the pharmaceutical and telecom industries consolidated to capture improved product pipelines and product development processes; for example, American Home Products acquired Monsanto to improve profitability through a pipeline of innovative products at Monsanto. In addition to the actual product pipeline, the company was purchasing a new product development process.

R&D product development cycle time, which results in first-to-market products, may create an almost insurmountable advantage in high-tech or highly competitive markets. Business development cycle times that are reduced may prove to be extraordinary advantages for acquiring companies. The acquisition of Chrysler by Daimler-Benz will add the rapid product development process to Mercedes if the integration is effectively managed, expand the Mercedes product lines (to lower-cost vehicles), and extend geographic presence within the U.S. markets. If process is a primary reason for the action, it is important to focus the review on process, sustainability, and transferability. Carefully review processes in the due diligence review to *ensure results can be duplicated in or transferred to the new company.*

Sales Process

Sales process can vary significantly within an industry. During 1997, Compaq's strategic analysis apparently identified that the company had a weak service position compared to HP and IBM. A review of the computer marketplace identified a floundering company—Digital Equipment Co.

(DEC)—which had a new alpha chip (which can be used in PCs and work-stations) and a very strong service organization. The sales/service organization at DEC represented a unique acquisition opportunity for Compaq. The acquisition provided expanded sales operations—with service—that Compaq could not offer before the acquisition. DEC also was a bargain purchase by many standards due to its depressed stock price. Because of this process addition, Compaq now has a more complete product offering to businesses throughout the world.

Exhibit 2.2 identifies two of the critical success factors for Compaq in the marketplace: global distribution effectiveness and after-sales service. These represent judgments of relative market strength. Note the obvious differences at Compaq (preacquisition sales and service processes were minimal versus the competition's). Once DEC was acquired and effectively integrated, Compaq was larger and better rounded. Purchase of the sales/service process considered all elements that affect performance—organization, training, procedures/manuals, and support services—to ensure that the final objectives were achieved.

Manufacturing Process

Effective manufacturing and distribution processes create market value for organizations. Consider the current impact of the Dell "dock-to-production" model, which has redefined the computer production/logistics

EXHIBIT 2.2   Computer Manufacturer Target: Service Company

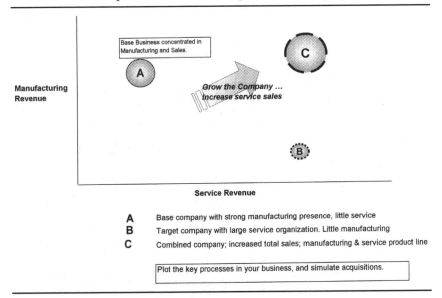

Note: The size of the sphere is relative to sales dollars.

environment and created an almost insurmountable competitive advantage. The customer order fulfillment cycle that Dell has created assures a cost advantage estimated at 9 percent in a low-margin business where total margins represent 20 to 30 percent.[5]

Manufacturing processes may be the most complex of any single functional area. Functions such as customer service, product design, inbound and outbound logistics, and manufacturing operations may be closely coordinated to improve customer satisfaction, eliminate waste, and improve productivity in a well-run company. As a result, acquiring and adapting improved manufacturing processes are difficult because of the complexity of the processes involved and the potential significant impact of a manufacturing shutdown due to integration failures. A complete review by manufacturing experts should be the basis of an effective evaluation of the process. Variables such as equipment (type and condition), workflow, manufacturing philosophy, procedures, and documentation must be carefully considered during the review. The quality of documentation must be carefully considered in manufacturing acquisitions, since, if relocated, the valuable insights that are not documented will be lost.

Manufacturing strategy or philosophy may vary from current "just in time (JIT)/synchronous flow methodology" to produce for storing in inventory. Manufacturing processes may be unique for each plant or facility, and longer-term or substantive change due to the physical characteristics of the separation of plants may be required. If integrated into an existing facility, process change in manufacturing will require physical plant changes and possibly unexpected additional investment. As you consider each manufacturing facility, your goal should be to migrate to the best practices, which may also require modifying your own processes.

Administrative Process

Administrative processes may be the source of competitive advantage in a business where service is the key. Such industries include insurance, banking, and health care. Administrative process can be viewed as similar to a manufacturing process. The product itself is processing transactions—entirely service oriented, with little tangible product output. Administrative process is critical to the livelihood of service companies. In 1997, Columbia HCA's rapid expansion caused a collapse of its business and stock price. The basic administrative infrastructure, such as data systems, communications links, procedures, policies, and personnel, was overwhelmed by the additional requirements of the many acquisitions. If Columbia HCA had better understood the impact of the dramatic growth of its business, the company likely would have included strategic acquisitions of administratively strong health care organizations or perhaps invested more heavily in the administrative process required to accommodate the high growth rate completed through acquisitions. Unfortunately, it considered "geographic or market share" growth to be its primary objective, possibly assuming that the processes would accommodate the growth. Integration of the operations appeared to be a critical need to create "cost advantage" and improved service while adhering to the high-quality service strategy. An ideal acquisition for this organization, rather than expanded market share, would be one that was administratively strong, was transferable, and had processes that were both sustainable and transferable.

Banc One suffered a similar result from years of acquisitions without effective integration of business processes, and as a result operates a very ineffective global business.

As a vestige of poorly integrated mergers, Banc One now runs seven deposit systems, three clearing networks, and five wire transfer platforms. Plus it needs separate maintenance contracts for each system, which are far more expensive than a single contract, and pays a king's ransom in software programming. Today the company spends 16% of non-interest expenses on computer systems. Wachovia and Wells Fargo, by contrast, spend around 10%.[6]

Apparently, as with Columbia HCA, Banc One's strategy focused on "top-line" growth with little consideration for effective service and competitive operating advantage.

Market Expansion

Products

In the telecom industry, acquisitions have occurred to ensure new product development and product line expansion. In 2003, Cisco acquired Linksys, a major wireless manufacturer. Linksys' products represent complementary products or product line extensions for the existing network product line. Product line extensions that are in complementary areas are easier to integrate since it is likely that manufacturing processes will be easier to integrate. Product line extensions may also lead to synergies when the acquired value chain is carefully reviewed, considering the value chain in the acquiring company.

Product line acquisitions may also be an expansion for the acquiring company. For example, in the 1980s Bausch & Lomb acquired the Charles River Breeding Laboratories. These products, while in the medical products market, did not directly impact the Bausch & Lomb product lines; there was no synergy. Historically, Bausch & Lomb product distribution channels included doctors, retailers, and consumer goods distributors. The acquisition represented a venture into genetics and animal breeding—an entirely new business segment for the company. This acquisition formed the base of operations in an entirely new strategic product line. Most likely the review process did not consider full integration, only a valuation of future business prospects in the new line.

Product expansion can be visualized through product mapping. Of course, as with all definition exercises, activity should be prioritized. Exhibit 2.3 reflects a simple summary of the existing and future products of two companies. The maps can be used to depict any significant information—for example, number of products, type of products, resources used, sales, gross profits, or contribution margin. The maps are a summary of product families, with products identified on the vertical axis. The horizontal axis is time, in whatever periods make sense (months, quarters, years). Time will vary based on the needs of the integration. For example, high-tech product integration would use shorter time frames more closely matching the product life cycle. Once the map is defined, areas of critical concern should be easily identified.

As these analyses are completed, you should avoid too much detail, or the real business issues will not be identified. Generally, limit the number of items to ten, or the process will become too fragmented and ineffective. If the product mapping or reason to acquire markets cannot be easily completed, more analysis and focus may be required in your M&A strategy. In Exhibit 2.3, new products to be acquired include both service and manufactured products. Note that the expected future service contract and flat panel displays have been targeted as priorities. If service is a major change in product offerings for the acquiring company, will the sales cycle differ? What information technology requirement will exist? Will additional training be required?

Market share is often a target for acquisition. Examples can be found in the automotive (GM's purchase of SAAB and Ford's acquisition of Jaguar), telecom (Worldcom's acquisition of MCI), and computer (SUN's purchase of Cray Computers) industries. In the cases cited, the market share increase is a niche within the overall market—such as Ford buying ultra-luxury cars. As these acquisitions are investigated, the acquiring company no doubt expects to achieve a certain level of synergy. Financial advantage through synergy can be developed through process enhancements (improving the quality processes at Jaguar), cost leveraging (distribution through the Ford/Lincoln dealer networks), cost reductions (transfer of design and manufacturing processes from Ford to Jaguar, and/or buying leverage for outside services such as advertising), or gaining leverage for existing infrastructure (cost-averaging in areas such as creative marketing, which may be limited at Jaguar).

Expanded geography may also be a target for market expansion. Geographic expansion requires further analysis to determine if the acquisition is to add geography or enhance existing coverage. Each of these purposes will have different challenges. For example, when a company acquires European operations to add geography, an improved understanding of laws, customs, and management styles in the region will be needed. Local

EXHIBIT 2.3   Product Mapping Worksheet: Sales (Millions $)

	Priority	Parent Company					Target Company					Integrated Company				
		Current Year	Future Years 1	2	3	Cumulative	Current Year	Future Years 1	2	3	Cumulative	Current Year	Future Years 1	2	3	Cumulative
Existing Products																
Manufactured Product																
Hardware																
Soundboard	C	10	10	10	3	23		25	35	60	120	10	35	45	63	143
Video Monitor 15"	C	22	22	5	0	27		3	4	4	11	22	25	9	4	38
Video Monitor 17"	C	5	5	16	16	37						5	5	16	16	37
Software	C											0	0	0	0	0
Services																
Service Contracts	B	10	15	15	20	50						10	15	15	20	50
Future Products																
Manufactured Product																
Hardware																
Soundboard - Digital	A							15	50	(100)	(165)	0	15	50	100	165
Video Flat Panel 15"	A	0	5	7	15	27						15	5	7	15	27
Video Flat Panel 17"	A	0	7	9	12	28						5	7	9	12	28
Services																
Service Contracts	A	0	10	20	25	55						0	10	20	25	55

Note: As these tables are developed, major risk or opportunity areas can be highlighted to improve their visibility. As key areas are identified, summaries of issues to be considered in any transitional plans can be developed. These might include key personnel, patents, organizations and processes.

regulation may result in more business exposure, which can be reduced using the expertise of outside consultants. For example, in some countries informal distributor arrangements carry a very large legal obligation when terminated by a major company. If geographic expansion is done to improve coverage in an existing territory, the buyer may face new challenges to integration. Complementary coverage may be a more difficult transition due to the possible duplicate workforce and infrastructure and due to existing organizations, policies, processes, and informal customs.

The telecom industry has frequently expanded geography. The acquisition of MCI by Worldcom provided a blend of advantages for Worldcom. In addition to the products—such as local lines maintained by MCI—the company also acquired geography such as increased long-distance territory coverage. Worldcom has also acquired products in the form of fiber-optic distribution systems, which can be extremely expensive and time-consuming to install.

Geographic expansions may require little integration if the acquisition is additional market coverage. In 2002, South African Breweries PLC (SAB) announced plans to acquire Miller Brewing from Phillip Morris Cos. SAB, with current global sales of $4.2 billion, would become the world's third largest brewer. This acquisition expands its market reach to the United States and includes the number two U.S. distribution network for beer, which provides a boost to its premium Czech beer Pilsner Urquell that is now imported to the United States. SAB will also gain access to a more global currency—the U.S. dollar.[7] It seems that this acquisition will provide many benefits with minimal integration risk.

Geographic expansion may require limited integration: Only coordination about the goals at the senior level and minimal policy changes may be required.

A new study finds that some transactions are more likely to succeed: transatlantic mergers.

The research, by Mercer Consulting Group, examined 152 deals valued at $500 million or more from 1994 through mid-1999 in which a European company purchased a U.S. business or vice versa. The consultants tracked the share price of the buyer from a month before the transaction was announced to 24 months later. They then compared it with the share prices of their competitors over the same 25-month period. By this measure, 82 of the companies making an acquisition, or 54%, outperformed their rivals, far better than the usual success ratio of U.S. domestic or intra-European deals.

One reason transatlantic buyers beat the odds, says lead author Michael L. Lovdal of Mercer Management Consulting, is because many such deals were designed to expand geographic reach. As a result, there was less need for emphasis on cutting costs by merging overlapping operations, which can be disruptive and often hurts domestic takeovers. In addition, because there were so many parties scrutinizing the transactions—from antitrust regulators on both sides of the ocean to government and union shareholders in Europe—managers pursued only the most promising purchases. And finally, buyers worked much harder to integrate their new units, knowing in advance the culture clashes inherent in cross-border deals.[8]

However, if geographic expansion is complementary to existing operations, the integration process becomes more complex. A full evaluation of people, processes, and products will be required for both organizations to effectively integrate the acquisition. These considerations should be reviewed in the initial phases of the business review as well as throughout the due diligence review.

Depending on the type of benefit to be derived from the acquisition, the choice to integrate or not, the extent of process integration, and so on will determine the extent of due diligence planning and execution required.

People

Acquiring people is a very difficult business challenge—perhaps as difficult as changing the business process. People in an organization will have an existing culture: informal and formal organizations that get the job done. Integration of people can range from virtually no integration to a full integration to the acquiring company's organization, processes, and business methods. Culture may include factors such as risk tolerance, approval structures and authority, and communications. Consider how the extremes of any of these topics may clash if they are inconsistent among the combining companies. Personal sensitivities may be high, and the acquisition transition must be handled very carefully.

Cisco Systems Co. has acquired many companies since 1993 and spent more than $5 billion focused on synergies of additional products through the well-developed Cisco sales and marketing organization. Cisco has very specific criteria for identifying acquisitions. Generally, acquisitions share the same philosophy and culture as Cisco. John Chambers, CEO of Cisco, summarized their philosophy briefly as follows:

As I mentioned, we are in the business of acquiring people. That is different from the automotive or financial industries, where you are acquiring process, customer base, and distribution. So when we acquire something, we are not acquiring distribution capabilities or manufacturing expertise. We—Cisco—are very good at that. We are acquiring technology. In this business, if you are acquiring technology, you are acquiring people.

That is the reason large companies that have acquired technology companies have failed. If you look at AT&T and NCR, or IBM with ROLM, the acquirer did not understand that it was acquiring people and a culture. If you do not have a culture that quickly embraces the new acquisition, if you are not careful in the selection process, then the odds are high that your acquisition will fail.[9]

General Electric (GE) generally imposes its culture on the acquired organization. General Electric has a reputation for high-quality performance as well as good process and open communication. These advantages are well worth imposing on any acquired company. However, GE will not make hostile takeovers, since the result will be an ineffective culture transfer.[10]

A "people" acquisition requires a thorough understanding of who the key people are and why they are critical. These are not quantitative exercises, but they will require "soft" research. There will be no balance sheets to examine, no physical assets to value, and no project plans to review. However, people may well be the key to the successful integration.

Soft research, such as observation of the organization, interviews, and informal crosschecks, will allow assessment of the people in the business. Once an acquisition is confirmed as a people acquisition, it is important to identify key people and to understand what is required to keep them as employees—through direct questions, observations, trial proposals, and negotiations. People acquisitions are very difficult to manage successfully, since people are very complex.

In many industries, people are the keys to the success of a business. High-tech industries are often driven by the brilliance of key personnel. These experts have a unique market position: They are in demand, and they often get what they want. As companies acquire entrepreneurial firms, cultural changes may be made to accommodate the needs and demands of essential employees. Acquiring companies may change organizational standards to accommodate culture change for these entrepreneurial acquisitions—for example, they may allow pets to accompany individuals to the workplace or provide game rooms for employees. These key individuals may be essential to the new product development process as well as to market position. An acquiring company may target a small or developing company for its personnel. Think about the impact on the due diligence review process and the initial integration process if people were the main reason—the value added—for the acquisition. Would the reviewers be more sensitive to the personal needs and desires of the employees? Would the review require a different review team? Would they approach the review strictly from a technical content point of view rather than a typical organizational review? Would the team try to "sell" the acquiring company more if an individual were key?

Financial

Acquisitions for financial reasons may include *diversity of the business cycle* or *economies of scale for financial reasons.* Diversity of the business cycle will allow organizations to legitimately smooth performance across various business cycles. As certain business cycles decline, others will improve. In the late 1980s, for example, Xerox acquired the insurance organization Crum & Foster. This was done to diversify the Xerox business cycle and ensure continued steady growth of sales, earnings, and shareholders' value. However, there was little in common between the two businesses. There were no similarities in manufacturing, logistics, administration, or

legal or regulatory environments. Eventually, Xerox determined that the off-
setting cyclical benefits did not offset the cost of the diversification. In early
1998, Xerox divested one of its last remaining pieces of the Crum & Foster
insurance organization. Xerox determined that the diversification was not a
good use of its strategic resources and refocused on the digital office.

In the mid 1980s, Bausch & Lomb reoriented its business strategy from
one primarily of industrial products and optics to one focused on medical
products. It completed this transition through mergers and acquisitions.

Scale of business may also be an excellent reason to acquire companies.
Al Dunlap has used scale, most recently in the acquisitions of Coleman,
First Alert, and Mr. Coffee, announced in early 1998. His strategic intent
for these acquisitions was cost elimination or reduction of unnecessary
overhead in the consolidated organization.

Dunlap is setting aggressive margin targets of 20%—far above Coleman's historic
high of 13.4%. That would probably mean additional cuts in Coleman's product
line. In addition, Levin says, Sunbeam may move some of its manufacturing to
Coleman's Wichita plant and close more of Sunbeam's facilities. "They are going
to do things we couldn't do on our own," he says. Sunbeam also expects to use
Coleman's overseas distribution channels for its wares.

Dunlap is out to prove that Coleman can be a useful tool in his rucksack as he
builds a global consumer-products company. That's probably bad news for many
Coleman workers.[11]

Sales, administrative, and marketing organizations—and possibly the
entire infrastructure organization within the target company value chain—
may be eliminated in such an acquired company. As a substitute, Dunlap
would use the Sunbeam organization for these functions. He may also use
the manufacturing resources available at Sunbeam to manufacture product
lines acquired. In June 1998, Sunbeam terminated Al Dunlap, apparently
due to missed financial objectives. This, unfortunately, is a reflection and a
result of the hazards and complexity of combining operations.

General Electric has used scale to its advantage in many acquisitions.
The GE name, organization and structure, and purchasing power provide
for many cost savings and business leverage.

SHOULD WE INTEGRATE OR NOT?

A question related to any acquisition is "Integrate or not?" The question
must be answered, and action plans must be implemented to achieve the
goal. When there is no well-thought-out, well-defined strategy, the business may become dysfunctional. Banc One suffered such a fate after the
merger of Banc One and First Chicago NBD:

Consider the context for that transformation. Banc One is the product of a $29 bil-
lion 1998 merger between the old Banc One of Columbus, Ohio, a big retail outfit
in the Midwest and Southwest, and First Chicago NBD, a venerable corporate

bank with a long tradition of lending to medium-sized manufacturers. The deal posed the classic problem of mergers of equals: Neither side was in charge. "The two camps would argue for months over whether retail or corporate should get the big resources, which people from which former bank should run the businesses, and everything else," says Dave Donovan, head of human resources at Banc One and a veteran of First Chicago.

Banc One and First Chicago were products of multiple mergers of their own, yet they had failed to impose strong central control on the banks they'd bought. Different regions set their own guidelines for making loans, sewing a crazy quilt of credit standards. It seemed top management could agree on just one thing: Everyone wanted to grow revenues as rapidly as possible. The quickest route was piling on risky loans.

The pressure on lending was exacerbated by the need to make up for plunging profits at First USA, the credit card business that Banc One bought in 1997 for a lofty $8 billion. In the early days of the merger, First USA disastrously mistreated its cardholders, bumping rates from 4.5%, say, to 19.9% if they paid even one day late on just two occasions. Customers departed in droves.[12]

Integration of companies can be extremely complex and risky. Risks are not limited to the acquired company but also may include the acquiring company. Financial results may strain the borrowing levels, cash flow, and earnings per share in the entire company. Integration is not a process that can be thoroughly planned in a short period, like a weekend. The *dimension* or broad strategic intent of the integration can be identified in a short time. The integration criteria must be thoroughly analyzed to provide management with a complete understanding and, where possible, quantification of the advantages of the integration process. Integration is always an expensive and complex process, but it may also be the best alternative to consider in the strategic intent. Integration should be carefully analyzed and consider:

- Estimated costs, including incremental capital and expense, total cost, and timing of spending
- Benefits: incremental, total, and timing
- Expected timeline for successful integration
- Risk analysis: priority and probability assessment
- Consider alternatives: managing separately, partial integration

Estimated Costs of Transition

Cost estimates should reflect the normal out-of-pocket costs such as attorneys, accountants, consultants, taxes, registrations, and the like. However, the costs should also include internal costs during the transition for inefficiency, training, process changes, relocations, and so on. The integration assessment should consider the current level of performance of the buying company and the costs required to raise the performance of the target company to a consistent level. Tolerance of reduced performance by the acquired company may reduce the value of the total company.

A master template including all generic cost categories that may be incurred in a transition will help ensure that all acquisitions are evaluated consistently and that all potential costs have been considered. It is best to prepare such a matrix before an acquisition is in process, rather than try to develop one ad hoc during a negotiation. Note that in Exhibit 2.4, both the type and the timing of costs are identified. The detail is important to estimate the balance sheet and cash flow, impact on future operations, and P&L impact on a periodic basis.

EXHIBIT 2.4   Integration Planning Costs and Capital (Millions $)

Type of Cost	Total Costs			Monthly	Notes
	Estimate	Minimum	Maximum	Run Rate	
P&L					
Base Costs					
Legal					
Fees	0.5	0.3	0.7	0.2	A
Travel	0.1	0.1	0.1	0.1	
Registrations/filings	0.1	0.1	0.1		
Licenses	0.1	0.1	0.1		
Finance					
Fees	0.3	0.2	0.4	0.1	
Travel	0.1	0.1	0.1		
Registrations	0.1	0.1	0.1		
Manufacturing					
Engineering	0.4	0.3	0.8	0.1	
Temporaries	0.3	0.3	0.4	0.1	
Inefficiencies					
Manufacturing	1.5	1.0	2.0	0.5	B
Distribution	0.2	0.2	0.3		
MIS	0.3	0.3	0.8	0.1	
Total P&L - Costs	**4.0**	**3.1**	**5.9**	**1.2**	
CAPITAL					
Software Licenses	0.2	-	0.5	n/a	
MIS - Hardware	0.4	0.2	1.5	n/a	
Total Capital	**0.6**	**0.2**	**2.0**		

Estimates are based on a 90 day transition for the integration.

A = Represents out-of-pocket costs for incremental legal... and monthly run rate if the process is prolonged.
B = Represents estimated lost efficiency due to key manufacturing personnel
    travel to target company & not attending to current schedule

Prepare initial estimates for valuation, and validate during the Due Diligence initial steps in the integration process.

Notes: (1) Estimates are very broad. Precision is not required, but there should be a reasonable level of accountability. (2) Monthly run rate will assist in comparison of trade-offs with out-of-pocket costs, compared to savings to accelerate the project. (3) Monthly run rate emphasizes dollar impact of delays. (4) Cost estimates will be prepared by the functional executive responsible for the area and will be used to measure performance. (5) Inefficiency can be a major cost and is often overlooked. This does not capture the market cost of disrupted customers. (6) Minimum/maximum estimated costs frame the potential impact of the entire transaction. (7) Capital estimates assist in cash flow planning.

There are several important components within Exhibit 2.4:

- *Type of cost* includes *base costs* and *inefficiencies*. Base costs represent the out-of-pocket spending required to effectively complete an acquisition. Out-of-pocket costs include such standard items as legal, accounting, fiscal registrations, outside consultants, equipment repair/abandonment, training and so on. Responsible members of the acquisition team should develop these costs. Inefficiency represents the estimated costs resulting from the turmoil of the integration process, and this should consider all company activities. Costs such as maintaining duplicate information systems may actually increase as the delay continues. When you consider the total inefficiency of two entire companies, these costs are significant. This is yet another reason for a quick integration process.

- *Minimum and maximum estimates* are prepared by knowledgeable representatives to bracket the decision within a range of least to most significant cost for the activity. As cost estimates are prepared, hi-low cost bracketing should be used to develop a best-case/worst-case summary of the acquisition transaction. While "cost bracketing" is not a precise valuation process, it will provide a better framework for the acquisition decisions. If, at the extremes, the acquisition costs are reasonable enough to proceed, further work may not be required. If initial cost estimates are excessive, more analysis can be completed. During the estimating process, it is essential that *the functional executives—for example, marketing, operations, finance, and so on—be accountable* for the estimate. As the cost of the transaction is summarized, maximum costs may require close review to ensure that the economic justification is still valid. If maximum costs are significantly higher than is acceptable, a change in plans may be required.

- *Run rates* are the spending levels per period—for example, one month or one quarter. These will assist to develop the spending trade-off necessary in the decision making to spend more incremental costs to accelerate the integration process. If there are highly variable run rates, more monthly detail should be prepared.

- *Capital costs* incurred to effectively integrate the operations. Facilities and equipment costs may be required to integrate and properly size the company to the buyer standard. Process upgrades should be reflected in all cost estimates.

The due diligence process may focus on equipment serviceability, deviation from established standard equipment (e.g., mainframe-based software versus Unix-based distributed software), or lack of proper equipment. For example, in many small companies, something as simple as nonstandard PC equipment may cost hundreds of thousands of dollars to upgrade. Companies may not consider this inefficiency during the transition. Estimated productivity losses during the transition period can be as much as 20–50 percent when going through large-scale change.[13] The longer the transition process continues, the higher the transition costs. Note the magnitude of cumulative costs in Exhibit 2.5 due to inefficiency. As opportunities for transition improvement are evaluated, management should consider this hidden inefficiency cost in the decision process.

EXHIBIT 2.5 Total Integration Costs

Costs: Inefficiency + Out-of-pocket

Month	Cost (Millions $)	Cumulative: No Consultants
1	2.5	2.5
2	2.5	5.0
3	2.5	7.5
4	2.8	10.3
5	2.9	13.2
6	3.0	16.2

Costs: Inefficiency + Out-of-pocket

Month	Costs—No Consultants		Costs—With Consultants	
	Monthly Cost	Cumulative: No Consultants	Monthly Cost	Cumulative: Incl. Consultants
	(Millions $)			
1	2.5	2.5	3	3.0
2	2.5	5.0	3	6.0
3	2.5	7.5	3	9.0
4	2.8	10.3	1.5	10.5
5	2.9	13.2	1	11.5
6	3.0	16.2	0.5	12.0

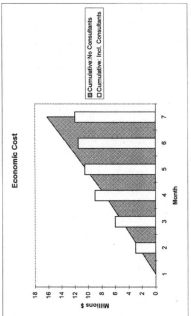

Economic Cost

■ Cost
▧ Cumulative: No Consultants

Economic Cost

▧ Cumulative: No Consultants
□ Cumulative: Incl. Consultants

Organization inefficiencies add up quickly - consider accelerating the integration process with outside consultants.

Cost estimates should be developed by the transition team, and they should be a firm commitment by the team and the leader. All costs for the transition should be considered in this estimate. In order to get to the cost estimate level of planning, teams and leaders must understand the result of integration or the "to be" organization. Cost estimates and timetables are necessary to complete the proper accounting for the transaction. One-time charges and capitalized costs should be identified during the planning process. Early identification of costs and major activities will allow for review and approval by management and for progress reporting against the objectives. The acquiring company would not want current-period earnings to be affected by having one-time transition costs erroneously included in the operating results. In addition, by keeping the cost estimates at a macro basis, the company can more easily estimate the value of alternative plans.

Integration executives should also be aware of the "opportunity cost" for long delays in integration. Opportunity costs may include lost customers, disillusioned customers requiring sales/marketing efforts, product introduction delays, and the like. Some studies indicate that the cost of acquiring a customer is 3–5 times the cost of maintaining a good relationship with a current customer. During periods of integration and major change in a company, the likelihood of customer dissatisfaction is increased dramatically. Can you afford to ignore or minimize that potential?

The examples in Exhibit 2.5 reflect how quickly costs accumulate for delays in completing the integration process. Inefficiency and run rate costs relate directly to the time required to complete the task. Inefficiency can only be estimated—but note its size in the example. Inefficiency may be one of the largest costs in the acquisition process, when you consider inefficiency in the 40–50 percent range impacting both companies.

Period cost run rates can be very helpful in managing the transition process. As the transition continues, decision trade-offs can be determined, considering out-of-pocket costs to accelerate the process versus the cost of delay. As an example, using only in-house engineers may extend the company manufacturing transition process by three months and increase total costs. In Exhibit 2.5, the total is $16.2 million of cost. An alternative to exclusively staffing through in-house engineering would be to use outside consultants. A company could spend up to $500,000 or more per month to accelerate the transition, and the company would economically break even. It is not just the financial costs that lead to "integration failure," but delays in integration will also erode morale and jeopardize any goodwill generated by the transaction. Separate lines should be added for significant one-time costs, such as severance, relocation, and outside consultants (e.g., MIS and engineering).

Benefits can include cost savings and sales and margin improvements.

Benefits: Cost Synergy

Synergy can be achieved by gaining more market presence or business advantage from fewer resources. For example, the 2002 merger of Compaq Computer with Hewlett-Packard expects to realize substantial cost savings as a result of the merger. "The CEOs said there will be real cost savings that will create efficiencies in the long run. They said they plan to slash 15,000 jobs, or 10%, at the combined entity, and will see cost savings of $2.5 billion by 2004."[14] As of December 2002, HP was one year ahead of schedule, by realizing $2.4 billion of annual savings out of an expected $3.0 billion.[15]

The benefits of synergy can best be analyzed only after the value chain (a summary of all the functional activities to serve the customers and manage the business) has been reviewed. The value chain analysis should reflect the components of each business based on the strategic plan to optimize the business after reconstruction. The strategic analysis should be completed in broad terms. For example, in a company with $100 million of sales, the nearest million dollars would be an appropriate judgment as these areas are initially assessed.

Macro estimates of cost savings to be achieved (e.g., through elimination of a department in the combined operation or a simple reduction of redundant functions) and confirmation that the required level of service can be delivered must be made by the integration team. This initial information would be obtained in preliminary financial analyses or during the due diligence review. If synergy savings are expected, accountability should be assigned to specific individuals. Without specific goals, synergy is an elusive target at best, and at its worst it becomes an indefensible goal that drains the energy of the integration team.

Note that Exhibit 2.6 is specific in both value and the name of an individual responsible for cost reductions. Ideally, the plan will include specific actions, timelines, and contingency performance plans.

Benefits: Sales Synergy

Companies are often acquired due to expected sales synergy. Complementary product lines may provide a distribution channel at virtually no incremental cost. The 1998 merger of Citibank and Travelers Insurance was expected to provide improved service to each client base and increased sales of both lines.

Sales synergy is often a goal of an acquisition, but many times it is not realized. *Business performance metrics should be established pre- or postintegration* to provide a benchmark for companies. Performance metrics can include sales or margin per headcount, gross margin rates, and changes in sales growth rates. These synergies should be used to justify the acquisition. As with all transition items, it is essential that the personnel establishing the estimates be responsible for their execution.

EXHIBIT 2.6 Company Synergy Acquisition Analysis: Company A + Company B (Millions $)

Description	Company			New Company	Notes	Responsibility
	A	B	A+B			
Operating Assets (Net of Depreciation)	450.0	700.0	1,150.0	900.0	1	Manufacturing
Employees	350.0	400.0	750.0	600.0		
P&L						
Sales	700.0	900.0	1,600.0	1,450.0	2	Sales
Gross Profit	400.0	600.0	1,000.0	1,000.0	3	Manufacturing
% to Sales	57%	67%	63%	69%		
Expenses						
Selling	75.0	150.0	225.0	200.0		
Marketing	75.0	75.0	150.0	125.0	4	Marketing
R&D	70.0	120.0	190.0	200.0		
Administration	45.0	60.0	105.0	75.0	5	Finance
Total Expenses	265.0	405.0	670.0	600.0		
Pretax Earnings	135.0	195.0	330.0	400.0		

This chart represents a financial summary of the benefits of synergy. The ideal method to size the company is to look at the industry, products, processes, and determine the best company of the future - the "to be." Review should not be influenced by the composition or structure of the current company. You must define the ideal company after all the consolidation and integration is completed the to be state.

Notes: 1 = Disposition of the LA manufacturing facility; 2 = vice president of sales to eliminate products with sales less than $1 million and gross margin of less than 30%; 3 = manufacturing to eliminate the LA manufacturing facility and 150 employees; 4 = marketing to eliminate PR in the target company; and 5 = finance to eliminate duplicate MIS function.

Goodwill or Reputation

A company's reputation may be a good reason to integrate the organization. Companies with good products but poor reputations may be value-priced and perfect acquisitions. Depending on the size of the company, a small acquisition may actually improve company valuation due to the "halo effect" of the larger acquirer. Advantages and disadvantages may occur as a result of the integration depending on the resulting dominant organization and its reputation. Integration could be a disadvantage, however, if the acquired company dilutes the reputation or effectiveness of the acquirer. Recall that the poor quality of Packard Bell's PCs continued to plague the company even after NEC acquired the company. Poor quality and aggressive competition resulted in market share loss during the second quarter of 1998.[16] During the next few years, NEC ceased to be a major competitor in the PC market.

A company's reputation rests on values and performance as delivered by the employees. As high-quality companies acquire others, there may be a halo effect in the near term. Effective integration of values, policies, and processes will continue the high value of the acquisition.

Timeline/Planning

Planning either for a full or partial integration or for managing the companies separately is critical. Timelines and cost estimates for each major activity should be prepared, with individuals responsible to perform the activities. Broad cost comparisons should be developed for the alternatives. It is very important to ensure that the project is tightly controlled and well planned. When acquisitions are significant, these plans should be reviewed and approved by both senior management and the board of directors. Transition timing will depend on potential value gains and costs driven by the integration process. Timing must be carefully coordinated among the companies, organizations, and people, and should consider all the constituents. Each of these factors will be considered in more depth in later sections of this book. If the transition team loses control of the process, the acquisition may become exceptionally expensive—both as an activity and to the company stock valuation. Recall that at Danka Business Systems PLC, nearly one-third of the market value of the company was lost in a single morning's trading in the late 1990s due to delayed integration of the Eastman Kodak copier operation.

Risk Analysis

All plans should be assessed to determine the probability of successful completion. Risks must be reviewed with senior management in both companies. Major or critical path activities should have contingency plans in place to reasonably manage missed objectives. The risk analysis should focus on the critical elements of value—people, process, customers, and so on—to ensure that the basic investment is effectively managed.

Periodic reporting concentrating on critical planning elements and their costs should be prepared by the integration team to ensure proper oversight. Reporting and informal communications should be more frequent initially to ensure that all major issues have surfaced and that the team is capable of the integration task.

SHOULD WE MANAGE SEPARATELY?

There may be advantages for keeping separate products or companies. When cultures, organizations, or product lines or businesses differ significantly, the greatest value may be captured through separate management. Examples include Bausch & Lomb's acquisition of the Charles River Breeding Laboratories or the Xerox acquisition of Crum & Forster. Clearly, Bausch & Lomb and Xerox were extending their product offerings and adding a strategic platform for growth when virtually no synergy or combination benefit would result. The goal of managing separately should be established as the deal is structured and justified.

A company acquisition without integration requires the same preliminary analysis, except that the final conclusion may be to maintain separate businesses. Definition of purpose, analysis of costs, benefits, and organization and constituent impact will justify the final decision. The analysis should be completed to ensure that there are no unsupported, preconceived commitments made. Review of personnel, product lines, and facilities may only require a cursory review, but once completed the leadership will know the conclusion.

QUICK CHECK OF CHAPTER 2

✓ Understand purpose
✓ Focus on critical success factors
✓ Define "as is"
✓ Define "to be"
✓ Understand costs and benefits

3

Due Diligence/Integration Process: Key Elements of the Deal

The acquisition should serve a purpose: Increase stockholder value through a specific strategy. The due diligence review will validate that purpose or raise issues that may require additional fact-finding or negotiation. The due diligence review process is essential in all acquisitions. *A team of seasoned experts who understand the strategic intent of the acquisition should complete the due diligence review process.* The team should become familiar with the strategic plan, the strategic intent, and the critical success factors as defined in the company's strategic plan, and with the goals for the target company. The due diligence team leader should be a senior member of the acquiring organization who has the authority to direct the integration activity and make decisions and judgments in the off-site review. Team members should understand that the purpose of the due diligence review is to observe and assemble enough information to make a good investment decision about the acquisition, valuation, and compatibility of the company, organization, personnel, or product.

This chapter will not discuss all the components of the due diligence process but rather will serve as a guideline to identify critical issues during the process. It is important to recognize that the due diligence team is responsible and accountable to complete these review areas. Failure to complete an effective due diligence review may cause an excellent deal to be rejected or a bad deal to be completed. *This is not just a technical review of P&Ls, balance sheets, cash flows, headcount, square footage, and so on but also should be a comprehensive business review of all significant business facets that will serve as a foundation for the integration process.* The review should be based on the buying company's standards—those performance policies that the company lives with every day—of normal operations and routine policy in areas such as maintenance, training, and quality. The review should also carefully consider sustainability and transferability of processes, procedures, and organization. Buying a substandard company may seriously hurt the acquiring company, either through integration cost or disruption of processes to key constituents such as customers, vendors, or employees.

The due diligence review team should include functional experts that will complete the review based on the critical success factors identified for the acquisition, their functional business judgment, and their knowledge of how the acquiring company operates. The team should review the acquisition and be accountable to the review team leader and ultimately to the board of directors for the proper execution of due diligence/integration. Generally, due diligence review teams have lists of major items to be investigated. However, team members must understand that *their responsibility is to use judgment, observation, and technical skills* to identify issues that may affect valuation or the decision to buy.

Exhibit 3.1 reflects the broad interlocking responsibilities of the functions. Responsibilities overlap repeatedly among the functions—there are no rigid lines of narrowly defined accountability, but rather a cooperative spirit focused on the key elements of due diligence. As a team, the functions must review, assess, and plan the acquisition, and if done properly the team will also be responsible to execute the integration.

Some companies use acquisitions as a method to diversify the product lines and business risk. When companies expand beyond their core competency, they should consider hiring experts in the field to provide expert counsel and assistance in the due diligence review.

EXHIBIT 3.1   Due Diligence and Business Integration Team Efforts (Overlapping Responsibilities Focused on a Common Goal)

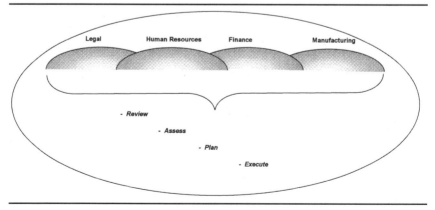

In addition to the technical issues that should be investigated, the team is also the first on-site intelligence for the intangible or qualitative assessment of the acquisition. The intangible review requires experience and judgment to understand the information observed. Judgment and clear unbiased observation are important elements of a successful due diligence review. Thinking beyond the norm or "outside the box" is essential in the due diligence review.

The due diligence review team has four main responsibilities:

• Validate the assumptions, which would include integration costs and cost/benefit assumptions used in the initial valuation of the acquisition.

• Define upsides to the purchase transaction based on preliminary information.

• Identify potential downsides to the transaction observed compared to assumptions used in the valuation and purchase assessment.

• Identify significant transition issues.

All significant variances from key assumptions in the deal structure and strategy should be immediately reviewed with the due diligence team leader.

Validation

The team leaders should summarize the essential elements of the deal. These could include components of valuation, company strategy, and assessment of assets, liabilities, contingent liabilities, personnel, products, and processes at the target company. These will vary with each acquisition transaction but *should be based on the strategic plan and critical success factors* necessary to enhance stockholder value. Critical success factors may be defined in many ways. An example is a rapid, validated new product development process (e.g., Chrysler can create a new auto in less than two years). The responsibility for the due diligence team in this case may be to validate the process and ensure its sustainability and transferability to Mercedes. After the team understands these critical success factors, the team should identify the steps required to validate the assumptions related to their functional area. The functional leaders should develop a step-by-step plan to effectively assess, in priority order, all elements of the acquisition, reflecting their functional and business judgment. Functional leaders in their management role must interpret their observations and modify their plan, if necessary, to thoroughly understand the key issues. As the review progresses, significant observations should be shared with other team members to ensure that the operation being acquired meets the strategic objectives. If there are major differences from expected key elements, the team leaders should assess the impact on the value of the deal. At the conclusion of the review, each functional leader should make a clear statement about the validity of the assumptions.

Upsides

Upsides to the transaction can include current benefits and strategic benefits (i.e., known new product development projects identified during the review that complement existing R&D projects in the acquiring company, manufacturing capacity immediately available not previously considered, and the like). During the review, communications among the functional leaders should be both structured (to discuss the scheduled review items) and free flowing to ensure that anything significant is considered in the review. Often, as the functions talk about findings, new upsides are identified. Unforeseen benefits can have an immediate, significant effect on the negotiations and financial evaluation when they represent more tangible, less risky opportunities. Communication with team leaders is essential. Upsides can be both near-term and strategic benefits.

Team members should use judgment to expand their review to factors that may be outside the original deal parameters. However, it is important that judgment drives the review—don't get distracted by insignificant factors. Reviewers should be wary of a search for value that will lead to much more investigation with little benefit. Ideally, team members will include mid- to high-level personnel. A word of caution: Reviewers should understand that if the target company were being actively marketed, target company personnel would describe the operation in the most positive view.

Unforeseen benefits should be reviewed carefully to ensure their validity and size. Again, teams can develop estimates based on "min-max-probable" criteria. Examples of such unforeseen benefits may include:

- Sales: New product lines not anticipated in the preliminary valuation. During the review, the "selling" organization often presents information in a favorable manner. Sellers will quickly identify upside opportunities that relate to new products or possibly new synergies in existing lines that may not have been considered in the initial valuation. During the review, the team should always search for upsides not previously considered, which may influence the valuation. For example, specific customer relationships may be identified that were also previously unknown.

- Manufacturing operations: Process improvements that can easily migrate to the acquiring company. During the review, manufacturing reps and engineers should search for unexpected advantages. Manufacturing process improvement, process setups, inventory control methods, and so on may be beneficial to the acquiring company. It is possible that relationships or contracts with specialty vendors will provide more benefit than originally expected. As these advantages are identified, it is important to remain within the spirit of any confidentiality agreements signed. If the deal is completed, it should be the responsibility of the manufacturing representative to implement any of the advantages identified. The team may also find software products used in unique ways, which would be beneficial to the acquirer.

- Marketing: Product synergies not originally anticipated due to unknown affiliations (i.e., pending co-marketing of consumer products with major companies such as Walt Disney Company).

- Other functional areas: The "soft" or internal side of business, such as training, management processes, and planning methods, may be identified during the due diligence review. If the team is constantly looking for advantages, many valuable observations can be obtained during a thorough due diligence review—some of which may have quantifiable benefit to the acquirer.

Downsides

Downsides to the proposed transaction should be identified as well and are the responsibility of all the team members. Downsides can include unforeseen problems that are current, near-term, or strategic and that may represent an unfavorable financial impact compared to the original valuation, including the costs to integrate. As the team reviews the business, they must consider the business environment. They should be observing, listening, and sharing information that may affect the buy decision with other reviewers. Examples of disclosures that may be important during the review include:

- *R&D business development timetables and accountability:* Management often requires that timetables for completing R&D projects should be established. Review teams should understand the effectiveness of the planning process and of timely project execution to the timetables. An R&D future product pipeline is often very important in the valuation. Experts should review the qualitative aspects of future projects and assess the validity of the schedule. Significant new product delays should be factored into the deal valuation.

- *Marketing programs* may have very favorable expectations. Again, review teams should understand the effectiveness of the planning process and of timely project execution to the timetables. Although not all companies document plans and expectations, an informal review with functional experts may reflect excessive optimism. Marketing failures or excessive optimism represent a downside to the acquisition.

- Data and communications systems are an essential component of a smoothly functioning organization. A comprehensive assessment of the qualitative—and not just technical—aspects of systems is essential. Smoothly functioning systems that provide timely, appropriate, and accurate information to the operations are critical during a transition period. In the late 1990s, companies were suffering with the "millennium bug"—systems that may not function effective 01/01/00. Major investments may have been required to upgrade systems to a functional status in the year 2000. In March 1997, a successful regional bank reportedly put itself "in play" because the amount of investment required for upgrading the data systems was prohibitive. Data and communication systems incompatibility may also represent major potential costs for successful business integration.

- Downsides may also include *governmental agency preliminary research, tax negotiations, and other legal and regulatory matters* that have not yet been officially documented. For example, during the past fifteen years, the U.S. government has concentrated heavily on compliance with environmental laws. While litigation may not yet be underway, correspondence may reflect pending issues. These should be pursued during the due diligence review.

Transition

Senior company executives and functional leaders in the due diligence team should be held accountable for the successful integration of the company to its designated final stage of integration. This is a deliberate decision, since accountability is essential to the acquisition and integration process. Identifying transitional or integration issues is critical during the due diligence review process. This early observation window will allow the acquiring company to properly assess preliminary assumptions and begin planning the integration. The most effective companies begin the "integration" process while still completing the due diligence process. Transition items consider all segments of the planning horizon: current, tactical, and strategic. The team members must identify immediate, near-term, and strategic issues. Transition elements include all significant issues that will accelerate or delay the timely integration of the companies. Transition issues can be both tangible and process oriented. The functional representative should identify transition items and, whenever possible, prepare an action plan to resolve the issues (including timetable, cost to resolve, and business impact if not resolved). Identifying transition issues early may define the ultimate success of the acquisition; also, delays cause up to 50 percent inefficiency during the transition. During the transition assessment, the team should consider sustainability and transferability of the processes, not only from the buyer to the target but also from the target to the buyer.

Cisco is noted for its swift, friendly, and very productive integration process. In a recent article by Booz, Allen & Hamilton consultants, they noted that there are several critical features to a Cisco acquisition:

- Vision
- Quick wins for the shareholders
- Long-term wins for all constituents
- Chemistry or culture must be right
- Geography (for large acquisitions)

Note that these five criteria are specific goals that must be achieved in any of their acquisitions. The criteria are inflexible, as discussed with John Chambers, CEO of Cisco, in *Strategy & Business:*

S&B: How disciplined are you in your approach to those five criteria? If they are not all in place, will you still buy a company if the technology is great or the people are very good?

John Chambers: No. We don't do it. We've killed nearly as many acquisitions as we've made. We killed acquisitions for those reasons even when they were very tempting. I believe it takes courage to walk away from a deal. It really does. You can get quite caught up in winning the acquisition and lose sight of what will make it successful. That's why we take such a disciplined approach.[17]

DUE DILIGENCE PROCESS

Due diligence should focus on "What is important?" It is very easy to automatically review checklists, check the boxes "complete," and not focus on important elements. It is important to avoid a mechanical review and to thoroughly understand the purpose of the acquisition.

The review process consists of a review of tangible and intangible items, and observation and analysis of the management process, the organization, and the people. Technical/tangible issues are generally outlined in a checklist managed by one of the team members who is a functional expert. In addition to the checklist, the expert must use judgment, understand the goals of due diligence and of the acquisition, and modify the review wherever appropriate.

The review process will validate that the target meets the criteria established in the initial valuation and planning process. Although the checklist is a detailed list of questions, it is important that *seasoned managers and executives complete the review to thoroughly understand the nuances of a business operation.*

An example of a due diligence review checklist is included in the Appendix. Regardless of the checklist used, a master checklist modified to reflect the critical success factors of a particular deal should be used on all acquisitions. The checklist should be organized by type of functional responsibility to make it easier to distribute among the team members. Initial team meetings should define the scope of the judgment to be used (e.g., no issues less than $100,000) as well as the communication responsibility for the review team members. Teams perform best when they have successfully completed the due diligence review process on a previous assignment. Close coordination and development of judgment is essential for the process to work effectively. The due diligence review process must include frequent meetings among the team members throughout the review. Functional team members generally work with their counterparts at the target company.

The review is a blend of formal interrogation, careful review of documentation, thorough assessment of essential issues, observation of the business, and informal discussion. At the conclusion of the review, the team should recommend either purchase or not, based on a comparison to the assumptions, and deal structure. The "buy" decision may also include exceptions or changes to the original valuation assumptions, which require price changes and concessions.

During the site visits, communications should be closely monitored due to the sensitivity of the review. Team members should understand the implications of their comments and questions during the process. It is important for the team to understand that being "sold" is very emotional for the acquired company employees. Target company employees may lack secure jobs or may be at risk in their compensation and/or benefits. Unguarded, informal conversations may cause problems with people at the target company and eventually disrupt the integration process. A casual statement may be misinterpreted or repeated out of context, establishing barriers to future communication or perhaps obstacles to successfully completing the deal. Team members should understand that they represent the "head office" of the acquiring company. Casual comments discussing closing plants, firing people, and the like should be avoided. Team members must complete the review, understanding that the results of the review will serve as the basis for one of the most significant company purchases ever made. If team members are not the functional heads of the organization, the team members should have access to functional heads at any time. Significant issues may be listed in a format as in Exhibit 3.2. Note that the worksheet establishes accountability, a description of the issue, a valuation, and a statement of resolution. These worksheets may be a critical element of the integration process.

Occasionally, if the company ventures outside its normal core competency, outside experts should be consulted to more effectively evaluate an acquisition. These outside experts must understand that the *due diligence team leader is responsible for the successful completion of the due diligence review process.* The leader must ensure that the *consultant has a*

EXHIBIT 3.2   Due Diligence Transition Issues: Company X

Function: Finance			Reference Issue: Responsible:
Timing:	Mark with X	Type Mark with X	Reviewed: Date Open:
Immediate		Validation	Resolved:
One Year		Upside	
One Year +		Downside	
		Transition	

Description of Issue

Resolution

thorough understanding of the transaction: elements of valuation, critical success factors, and so on. The expert must complete the technical checklist available as well as develop his or her own questions and business issues based on functional expertise. It may be necessary to bring in experts from legal, financial, accounting, human resources, or technical specialties (e.g., engineers and manufacturing representatives) to ensure that an effective acquisition due diligence review is completed.

A due diligence review checklist can be prepared by focusing on company financial statements, and the value chain of activities can serve as a checklist of major areas for review. As the framework is developed, time frames are a focal point—historical, present, and future. In each case, the assessment should consider the "business" nominal value and extent of change across the time periods. This framework should be amplified through a brainstorming session to include any topics considered necessary by the team in the due diligence review. The review session should be scheduled after completing a thorough review of the proposed transaction but before any on-site review. The review should include technical (or tangible) and intangible issues.

For example, if a reviewer were examining a deferred receivable with a value of $10 million, due diligence questions would include not only "Is the $10 million collectible today?" but also "Was the company involved in deferrals last year? If not, why do we now offer such terms? And will deferrals increase in the future due to deteriorating market conditions?" This accounting thread may lead to a marketing awareness of lower growth characteristics than expected. This thread may impact new product development spending and also change expectations of future revenue and gross profit. Exhibit 3.3 will provide a guideline to help assess the critical issues for a due diligence review.

Tangible

The technical or tangible review should include inspection and review of all tangible evidence that supports both the *immediate value* of the business (i.e., an appraisal of the assets such as inventory, fixed assets, and accounts receivable), and the *expected future value* of the business. For example, construction in process or R&D in process should be carefully evaluated to ensure that reasonable valuations are developed in the review. Consider that an incomplete "asset" does present risk variables such as:

- How much will it cost to complete?
- Will the design specifications be consistent with future needs?
- Will the asset perform as expected?
- Will asset performance be consistent with the new parent company's standards?

EXHIBIT 3.3 Due Diligence Checklist Development

Responsibility	Primary Topic	Subtopic	Valuation Current Future (Millions $)		Process Transition (Acceptable/Not)	
FINANCIAL STATEMENTS						
Finance	Cash	Demand Accounts US Dollars Foreign Exchange Time Deposits				Primary topics are defined by the project leader, and subtopics are developed in a brainstorming process. Each of the topics should be reviewed for the three primary due diligence issues - Valuation (current and future potential), Process Transfer, and Full Transition.
Finance	Accounts Receivable					
Materials Management	Inventory	Inventory Quantity Inventory Valuation Obsolescence Excess Stock Standard Cost				The Financial Statements and the Value Chain can be used to develop a master checklist for items to review. Responsibility for each area in the matrix should be assigned to someone on the Due Diligence Team.
VALUE CHAIN ASSESSMENT						
	Accounting	Cash Inventory Fixed Assets Depreciation				
	Financial Planning	Strategic Plan Budget Forecast				
	Sales	Spending				

Note: The checklist requires that the reviewers evaluate the current issues for the valuation impact and also prepare a qualitative assessment of the business process, its transferability, and its validity when compared to the acquirer's.

The review requires seasoned experts due to the serious implications of poor judgment. Ford Motor Company discovered that incremental millions were required to upgrade the manufacturing operation of Jaguar to a standard suitable for Ford's "JOB 1—quality." Existing assets require an additional assessment—their functional worth at the present. Although tangible assets will likely be valued at cost, a generally accepted accounting principles (GAAP) requirement, they may not be fully functional due to minimal preventive maintenance completed historically. *A proper assessment of their serviceability and comparison to the buying company's standards should be made before valuation and deal consummation.* Can you imagine an engineer's review of equipment with a conclusion of "equipment serviceable," then after completing the acquisition, the engineer recommends scrapping the equipment because it does not meet minimum manufacturing standards?

The technical issues that cause major concerns in any review are listed as topics within the due diligence checklists. These checklists may vary from industry to industry and among companies. However, the checklist in the Appendix details some broad topics that are universal. The topics generally include areas where facts, data, or conclusions can be presented and easily confirmed. "Facts" include procedures manuals, new product introduction timetables, product sales and customer lists, and accounting information such as product costs, spending, and budgets. In each of these areas, the target company is expected to be able to discuss the information in reasonable detail to assure the reviewer that it is in control of the process. *The review team must maintain control over all documents obtained during the review process* due to the likely "confidentiality" requirements of the transaction. If the deal is not completed, all workpapers generally must be returned to the target company or certified "destroyed." The reviewers should obtain enough information to answer the questions "Should the company be acquired? What price should be paid? What are the costs to effectively integrate?"

As technical issues are identified, the reviewer must carefully consider the impact on further review and the potential impact on the deal. If particularly sensitive areas are encountered, the reviewer should immediately discuss the issue with the team leader and be careful not to alarm the target company. For example, if the marketing reviewer has identified significant new product warranty returns—and new products are the main reason for the acquisition—the reviewer should immediately discuss the information with the manufacturing and engineering participants and with the team leader. Judgment and communication are essential to effectively manage the acquisition due diligence process. The "tangible" checklist review should consider all factors that may influence the transaction—that is, valuation, or integration, of the target.

Intangibles or Qualitative Review

Process

The review requires an understanding of the buying company's processes, competence, and performance standards. Companies should understand their strengths and weaknesses, and how they may want to change the target company. The intangible review requires judgment and experience to be effectively completed. The review requires observation of the functioning company in all phases of the business. The business value chain is an ideal checklist of activities for this review. Team members should understand the business process within the company—that is, observe the essential primary and secondary activities as they occur. Essential processes should be defined in the acquisition summary and strategic intent. If it is not possible to observe real-time activity, the reviewer should discuss the critical processes with the personnel responsible for the activity. The team member should review the information used to manage the functional area to understand the operational effectiveness. Probing, open-ended questions are useful in completing the intangible process review—for example, "If you had the chance, how would you change the inventory levels? How would you improve the purchasing process?"

As an acquisition is reviewed, the individual experts responsible for the functional area should identify processes in the areas affecting the critical success factors for the acquisition. When a business is complementary to the buyer, critical processes should be highlighted and compared to those of the acquiring company. Processes that are similar in type and quality require a lesser review. Those that are dramatically different (e.g., less controlled, poor quality, or dramatically improved quality) should be assessed to determine the probable outcome if an acquisition is completed. That is, will the processes be transferred because they represent improvements? Alternatively, will they be discontinued? Establishing a matrix as in Exhibit 3.4 can identify similarities and differences. The functional experts can rate compatibility of the essential procedures on a prioritized or A-B-C basis. It is important to understand that perfection is not the goal of the due diligence review, but rather identifying significant issues and costs is. As people are interviewed, reviewers should understand the strengths and weaknesses of the organization, people, and processes. The review should consider linkage among all functional departments of the buyer and of the target company as a priority of the review.

The reviewer should consider issues that will significantly affect *current business* as well as the *integration and long-term strategy*. The review should highlight only those critical items since the review process is often too quick to get into any depth. Due diligence reviews may provide insight into the culture. Culture can include a broad range of topics, which are discussed more thoroughly in Chapter 5.

EXHIBIT 3.4 Due Diligence Reviewer's Guideline

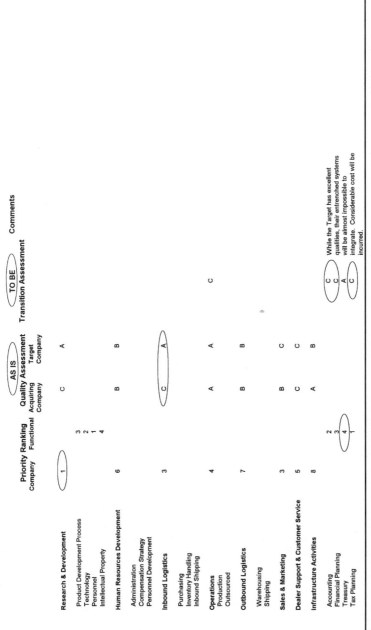

	Priority Ranking — Company	Priority Ranking — Functional	Quality Assessment AS IS — Acquiring Company	Quality Assessment AS IS — Target Company	Transition Assessment TO BE	Comments
Research & Development	(1)		C	A		
Product Development Process		3				
Technology		2				
Personnel		1				
Intellectual Property		4				
Human Resources Development	6		B	B		
Administration						
Compensation Strategy						
Personnel Development						
Inbound Logistics	3		(C)	(A)		
Purchasing						
Inventory Handling						
Inbound Shipping						
Operations	4		A	A	C	
Production						
Outsourced						
Outbound Logistics	7		B	B		
Warehousing						
Shipping						
Sales & Marketing	3		B	C		
Dealer Support & Customer Service	5		C	C		
Infrastructure Activities	8		A	B		
Accounting		2			C	While the Target has excellent qualities, their entrenched systems will be almost impossible to integrate. Considerable cost will be incurred.
Financial Planning		3			C	
Treasury		(4)			A	
Tax Planning		1			C	

Note: Ranking is a high-low ranking of the priority of the activity as a strategic imperative or regarding its importance to the long-range stockholder value increase. Subranking will rank the activity within the overall value chain activity. A ranking of "1" is most important—carefully manage all aspects of transition related to this area. In this example, it is obvious which activities are weak, and the benefits and detriments that will be realized when the target company is acquired. Points of extremes (e.g., "A" versus "C") should be carefully investigated in the preliminary and final due diligence review.

Legend:

A = Best; B = Acceptable; C = Unacceptable

Due diligence review team members must understand nonbusiness issues and the relationships among the different functions as they complete their business review. Factors that should concern all members of the team include organization, business process, morale, and creativity. These represent the intangibles or qualitative portions of the due diligence review. Understanding these issues will also help to define the challenges for integrating or combining the businesses acquired.

An effective method for focusing on critical process issues is shown in Exhibit 3.3. The checklist should be developed before the on-site review begins, and it should rank the areas based on the "to be" end state of the acquisition. This summarizes the primary and support activities for both the acquiring and the target company. The analysis should be prepared based on the acquiring company's strategic plan, and a preliminary assessment of the critical success factors should be identified for the target company. Summarization of these issues is judgmental and should not require hundred of hours of work to prepare. Accuracy is not essential, but rather a sense of the critical business processes is necessary. The primary and secondary activities should be ranked in priority from most important to least important (e.g., in high-tech companies, the most important function may be R&D, and the least important may be accounting). Subsets within the main activities should also be ranked within the category to provide some guidance to the reviewers. The companies should be "graded" by the team to ensure that reasonable assessments are obtained. "A" is the best, while "C" is the worst performance. Extreme evaluations—either very high or low—should be well understood to ensure that an effective review occurs and proper valuation and integration assessments are completed.

The purpose of this assessment is to focus the team on critical issues related to this particular transaction. Team assessments should be fair, but critical. The objective is to identify extremes.

Note how the presentation in Exhibit 3.4 easily focuses on the issues: R&D and inbound logistics are the keys to the acquisition, since the target is strong in each area but the acquirer is weak in them. Although other areas should be investigated, the key to the transaction is valid process assessment for R&D and inbound logistics.

As the reviewers complete their review, they should be wary of significant issues related to these two areas. "Soft" observations, such as high turnover, low morale, heavy overtime, extensive rework, and sloppy work areas, may be indications of serious process problems. Reviewers may also find that workers are highly motivated by the company's use of advanced, innovative motivational techniques such as recognition awards for high-quality performance, group problem-solving techniques, or "quality circles." These may also be particularly sensitive areas, since they may represent an area of significant competitive advantage. Therefore, the target company may be reluctant to disclose information related to these strengths.

Seasoned managers on the review team should be able to identify critical features of the process.

It is also important to understand the "negative" impact of acquiring a low-grade activity—note the poor performance of the sales marketing area in Exhibit 3.4. Reviewers should be aware of the extent of poor performance and attempt to determine the impact on the organization when consolidated or integrated. The impact could be cost, management dilution, and a resulting diminished business process in the acquiring company.

The intangible review also includes observing activity variances from official or documented channels. For example, procedures and organization charts may define a specific process to be followed for a transaction. However, essential activities may rely on "off-book" procedures. These can be identified during discussions and review of the reports. These excursions from official channels may also identify the critical people in the business process.

Management Reporting

Management reports should present the information necessary to effectively manage a company and should consider appropriate timing, content, audience, and frequency. Reporting is another observation window, reflecting how well a company is managed. Are the reports appropriate? Does management use them? Is the correct person receiving the report and using the information? As these questions are considered in the report review process by each member of the due diligence team, handwritten notes on the reports may indicate the quality and usefulness of the data. This will also be an ideal time to discover potential serious weaknesses in the management information systems. In poorly managed companies, numerous "Excel spreadsheet" summaries may indicate obsolete reporting processes, that require manual input of critical data. These manual iterations may be inaccurate and error prone, and may divert management's attention from the operating issues. For example, if a production report contains many reconciling items to reach the final value, the MIS system may require major changes or perhaps the controls over product movement are invalid. Seasoned functional experts will identify these problems and report to the group to determine if the problems are widespread.

Reporting may also provide insight into the quality of management. Effective reporting will be layered: the higher level in the organization, the more condensed and focused the reporting. Reports should include a hierarchy of information to reflect different levels of the decision process and responsibility. For example, if reporting is primarily alpha listings or part number listings, the company does not effectively manage information. The levels of enhanced reporting are reflected in Exhibit 3.5.

In effect, by understanding the critical success factors for the acquisition, the team members should be able to identify and scroll through the

EXHIBIT 3.5   Company Reporting: Basic and Enhanced Examples

Basic	Enhanced
Sales/Receivables Reporting	
Sales Territory Customer List	Sales Territory - Customer Aging
Total Accounts Receivable by Territory	DSO Metrics
Sales by Territory	DSO Graphs & Trends
Sales by Region	Narratives - Exception Reporting
	Trade Channel Summaries
	Hi-Lo Listings
	Gross Profit by Product
	Gross Profit by Customer
Inventory	
Inventory by Part Number	Inventory Turns
Inventory by Warehouse Location	Inventory Turns - Trends & Charts
Inventory by Plant	Inventory Turns - Product Class
	Inventory - Where Used Reports
	Hi-Lo Listings
	Inventory MOH

Enhanced reports disclose the management process - whether focused on the business drivers through management summaries or distracted and unfocused through extensive tabulations of facts.

primary and secondary activities to ensure that the essential activities are being effectively performed.

Preliminary Organization Review

The review process should include a preliminary review of the approved organization chart in relation to the business process. Each critical area should be thoroughly evaluated to ensure that it is as effective as expected in the valuations and that it functions as described in the documentation. If the process is different than either documented or expected, the reviewer must assess the quality of the existing process and, if adjustment is required, the extent of the problem, the amount of investment, and the time required to correct it. Preliminary interviews with personnel may identify organizational strengths and weaknesses, and the company culture. During the review, team members must observe the competence, leadership, and technical skill of the target company employees. Documented procedures and organizational responsibilities should be reviewed versus observed activity. Benefits and shortcomings within the organization should be noted and discussed with the team leader.

During this phase of the review, all team members should observe the company morale, cooperation among departments, and interaction with inside/outside contacts (vendors, customers, governmental agencies, and so on). These on-site observations will be critical insight into the operation of the company and will allow the reviewers to establish an opinion about the functionality of the company. All participants on the team should review the organization for these matters.

Organization Chart

The human resources representative is responsible for the formal organization review and should ultimately be responsible for a summary assessment of the organization. In addition to his or her own review, he or she must obtain assurance from other team members about the quality of the operations. The formal HR review should consider the fully staffed approved organization. The term "fully staffed" is used, since many organizations routinely have open positions and established part-time positions. Once again, it is important to understand the complete "as is" status. Factors that should be considered in the due diligence research include:

- An assessment of current organizational needs
- Assessment of the strategic human resources needs
- Identification of critical personnel and plans for retention during the negotiation process and the initial period after completion of the deal

Current organization needs should be separated into two categories:

1. What is necessary to manage the business today?
2. What is the current headcount status—for example, including temporary workers, open requisitions, and so on?

Definition of organizational requirements is the responsibility of each functional representative. As they review the respective functional areas, they should define organizational requirements, including number, type, and experience levels for all functions. This should be compared to the approved organization chart.

The organization assessment may include a review of the management process to control requisitions, open requisitions including specifications, job descriptions, and linkage within the organization. These documents are important indicators of the quality of an organization. Small businesses may not have extensive documentation, but a thorough understanding of the organization needs should be available. Based on discussions with key personnel, the reviewer should understand the current needs.

Existing strategic needs should relate to the target company's strategic plan. Often smaller companies do not prepare strategic plans, but rather think only in terms of increased near-term sales and additional plants or facilities. The acquiring company's due diligence team should assess stated strategic needs and consider the strategic requirements of the "to be" company. The assessment should also include a qualitative and quantitative review of the current organization. In addition to these assessments, the reviewer should *consider how or if the target company should be integrated into the operation*. Each significant conclusion should be documented and reviewed with the functional review leader and eventually the due diligence team leader.

Human resources is an ideal function to coordinate the personnel assessments of target company personnel. Formal and informal leaders in the target company should be identified and highlighted. HR management policies should also be considered as they relate to the buyer policies. Personnel matters (e.g., vacation policies, compensation, bonuses, and stock options) are extremely sensitive and could significantly affect the success of the integration. The HR representative will be an ideal person to try to categorize the culture of the target company.

Key People

Throughout this process, the team should identify key personnel. The identification process should be as thorough as time permits, based on a prioritized review. All personnel should be considered in the review to be sure that critical personnel have not been overlooked deep within the organization. If all personnel are not considered, how can you have that assurance? The HR team member should require all reviewers to develop a critical employee list, if any. The HR reviewer should have the prime responsibility to coordinate the personnel review, although other personnel will complete the technical review and assessment. This should include an assessment of skills, the critical nature of tasks to the corporation, and existing and possible future organizational structures once the company is acquired. Plans should also consider the soft side of people—for example, an individual's upward or horizontal mobility, and his or her willingness to relocate to a different city, if appropriate. As individuals are reviewed, personnel files should be available—although on a limited basis—to allow for a more complete assessment.

Critical personnel should be identified by the reviewers and communicated only to the senior team member or due diligence review team leader.

Names and brief biographies of critical personnel should be documented. Personnel may be critical due to their *impact on the leadership within the company, or due to technical skills that are essential to the company*. The reviewer should consider:

- Technical skills
- Educational achievements
- Company evaluation and achievements (such as patents, technical writing, etc.)
- Key projects in process
- Critical skills in management

- Relationships with key customers and suppliers
- Ethics and moral standards for those in leadership positions

In addition to the assessment of the individual, the format should include a critical assessment of the individual's true organizational impact. For example, organization charts may indicate certain reporting responsibilities but, in fact, individuals may function in a different manner or capacity. Do you recall the individual who worked in the plant for thirty years without fully documented manuals? He would know when a process was completed based on the sound of the machines and the rate of vibration on the floor. At precisely the right moment, he would release the flawless batch of product. The process could not be duplicated without his expertise, yet he was a relatively low-paid individual. Were those skills transferable? Will documentation be required to move the process? How many processes are actually completed according to the engineering specifications?

As critical personnel are identified and reviewed by the due diligence review team, preliminary decisions should be made to communicate with essential people about their future in the combined organization. Do not, however, communicate with any target company personnel without proper authorization from the HR leader in the due diligence/integration team. While no commitments can be made at this point because the transaction has not yet been completed, it is important to make people aware that their services will be needed in the combined operation. As key employees are identified, "golden handcuffs" (e.g., financial incentives that effectively commit essential people to the organization) may be appropriate. The target company generally does not provide such incentives until after the target company has completed the transaction, to avoid additional financial responsibilities. *Golden handcuffs should be offered only with the consent of the senior management at the target company.* Those who are not identified as "key employees" will know their status, so be aware of the impact on their future performance.

If restructuring is expected, study the target company culture and understand the implications on the overall company culture. Factors such as organized labor, existing company policies, and industry or regional tradition should be considered in any severance plans. The information should be used as the basis for planning transition cost. The objective is to plan out-of-pocket cost that is responsible, ethical, and reasonable. It is also important to understand that preliminary discussions about restructuring establish the tone for final negotiations in the acquisition process. For example, in a privately owned company, negotiations may stall if inadequate benefits or continued employment is not considered part of the overall transaction, due to the dedication of current owners.

Relationships

A relationship review may be necessary in the due diligence process. Essential relationships may include customer relationships, vendor relationships (although there may be no formal contracts, existing informal relationships should be understood prior to completion of the review), and other external relationships (such as distributors and government agencies).

Informal relationships, as mentioned earlier, may be considered official although not formalized in any procedures or organization charts. These relationships may be identified through review of correspondence, concentrations of invoices or payments, and discussion with responsible personnel. It is each reviewer's responsibility to thoroughly understand the business reality, rather than only the business that is documented and formally presented.

External relationships are important in the review process due to the constituents involved. Consider the impact on customers if suddenly another company—perhaps the main competitor—owns it. Consider the impact required for communication of items such as price lists, price changes, new product releases, and product updates on existing software. External relationships include customers, suppliers, vendors, government agencies, or any outside contacts maintained by the company in normal business operations, and they should be considered separately:

- Customers: In highly competitive industries, acquisitions may result with fierce competitors acquiring each other. Acquiring companies should understand the type of competitive conditions to effectively manage good customer relationships after the acquisition is completed. Customer lists should be carefully reviewed, analyzed, and prioritized to define a strategy to maximize the relationship once the deal is announced and completed.

- Suppliers: Without continued supplier relationships, the acquired company will not be successful. Major suppliers and critical or sole source suppliers should be identified, and relationships should be reviewed. This review will most likely be an informal process since documentation may not exist describing relationships. The senior materials management/logistics person on the due diligence team, working with both manufacturing and purchasing functions in the target company, would coordinate this portion of the review. Vendors should be prioritized in high-low listings or classified as A-B-C based on their importance to the company (e.g., technical requirements, geography, and breadth of product line).

In addition to suppliers, all major outside contacts should be considered in the due diligence review process. For example, government agencies may have ongoing discussions with the organization relating to things such as tax adjustments, EPA negotiations, and the like. These relationships should be considered as existing relationships in the acquiring company.

International relationships should be carefully reviewed. All international operations should be considered within the scope of the due diligence review. International acquisitions are more complex due to the varying laws, economies, currencies, and language requirements. In many international acquisitions, companies use outside experts to review their plans, strategies, and goals. Generally, Big Five public accounting firms, major international law firms, or other consulting organizations such as Booz, Allen, & Hamilton, and Bain and Company may consider the work within the scope of their practice. Often these individuals will review the due diligence checklist, as required by the purchasing companies, to insure that there are no significant adverse implications. It is important that these consultants be familiar with the strategic intent and near-term goals of the acquisition. It should be understood, however, that these individuals are experts in their function, rather than necessarily familiar with the acquiring company's operation. Certain items may be missed that only functional experts in the acquiring company would understand.

Based on the risks assumed in certain outside locations, it may not be necessary to visit each location personally. Small remote locations may not be priorities in the preliminary acquisition review, but be sure that you make a deliberate decision about the locations based on risk and opportunity and not just size.

Culture mapping, discussed in Chapter 5, will provide a basis for evaluating the acquisition's culture. This becomes very important as companies are merged, since studies have shown that most mergers fail to meet expectations—often because the cultures are significantly different and have not been effectively integrated.

Culture may vary by location, by type of industry, and by organization or function. In all cases, the cultures should be defined as completely as possible. Mapping allows the reviewer to identify intensity by function and steps within the organization. Locations may have differing cultures due to the type of management. Each of these can be adequately described and rated in a brief summary document. These documents should be reviewed and considered when developing the integration plan.

QUICK CHECK OF CHAPTER 3

✓ Keep the due diligence team for integration

✓ Validate assumptions early

✓ Define upsides/downsides

✓ Focus on critical success factors

✓ Standards of performance

✓ "To be" organization

✓ Key personnel/constituents

4

Communications: Guidelines for Strategy and Tactics

Effective communications about acquisitions are critical from the initial review through completing the acquisition. In publicly held companies, acquisitions must remain confidential to avoid artificial price changes in the acquired as well as the acquiring company, and also to avoid legal issues. Rumors and speculation can in fact ruin the deal. It is important that throughout the negotiation and completion of the acquisition, all communications be clear, concise, and properly scripted. All communication—whether formal or informal—should be carefully considered before public disclosure. Press releases, internal memos, and informal discussions with employees or third parties should be understood in the context of all constituents before their release. Generally, it is best to coordinate all *formal communication* through a single, trained, experienced individual to ensure that the message is consistent with deal tactics and strategy. Experience and deal knowledge will be a good foundation for a consistent message. It is also important to have seasoned, deal-knowledgeable executives working on the acquisitions, since it may often be impractical to formally approve all communications each time.

The designated communications coordinator should understand the temperament of the various audiences addressed as well as the expected emotional impact of the communication. Dealing with major stockholders requires a different sense than dealing with employees. For example, discussing potential restructuring of entire plants or functions carries very negative connotations to employees, while stockholders may perceive improved profits through better asset utilization. It is important that the tone and type of communication be carefully constructed and focused.

As with many activities involved in M&A, a communications strategy and plan will increase the probability of a successful integration. Communications should be planned around an anticipated timetable; acquisitions usually have at least a tentative activity schedule. This chapter will discuss the type of transactions and the timing/content of communications.

Written communications have longer visibility or endurance than verbal discussion, and if written communications are carefully developed they are less susceptible to misunderstanding. It is very important that these communications be properly reviewed, and it is particularly sensitive when public companies are involved, due to SEC regulation. Managing the communications process starts with the due diligence review. The due diligence review team members should become familiar with communications or discussion guidelines developed by the communications coordinator before the fieldwork is started. Specific briefs should be prepared to effectively respond to questions and concerns generally raised by target company employees and other constituents such as bankers, investors, customers, and suppliers. Each of these constituents may have a strong personal stake in the acquisition and must be considered in the communications strategy.

The coordinator may establish a guide to communications to outline topics for key team members, and include sections concentrating on constituents, timetables, or major strategies. Team members should assume that all public discussions and disclosures (including speeches, meetings, and other public forums) will be available to all constituents, the media, and, as a result, the competition. In fact, team members should assume that there are no secrets. If the acquisition is hostile, the plan should consider that the worst possible interpretation would be made to all disclosures, regardless of their intent. Plans to respond to these negative reactions should be developed prior to any such public disclosure of information. This may sound very conservative, but it is better to anticipate than to react.

TYPE OF TAKEOVER

Risks of successful integration change dramatically from hostile to desirable in public and private venues. Exhibit 4.1 depicts the extremes of risks based on type and size of acquisition—and the benefits of good planning when designing the communication strategy. Communications should consider the impact of the information and the risks associated with each type of disclosure.

The communications strategy and plan should be developed based on the type of acquisition and the impact on the constituents. As you might expect, a hostile public takeover requires the most careful communications planning due to the number of constituents, the emotion of the transaction,

EXHIBIT 4.1   Acquisition Risk Management

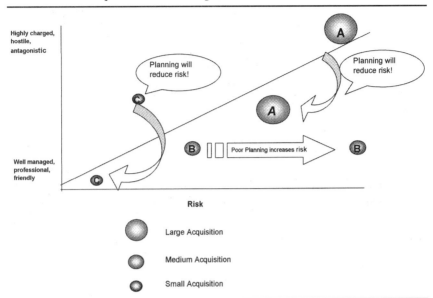

Note: By managing the activities and the overall communications process, it is possible to reduce the risk. Large, public, and highly visible acquisitions carry higher risks. Smaller private transactions are more easily managed and have less risk. Plan, execute, and continuously evaluate your progress.

and the potential impact on the constituents. Consider all the communications required of Compaq and HP during the merger discussions in 2002. Although the acquisition most likely did not proceed as smoothly as originally planned, it is virtually assured that once the process started offtrack, communication planning was critical to the final merger approval. All acquisitions should have a communications plan approved by the team leader, with periodic reporting against objectives.

Communications should be carefully constructed based on the type of takeover. Takeovers can be broadly classified as desirable, acceptable, or hostile to assist in developing the communications plan. It is important to review the acquisition components as well as the entire proposed acquisition in these terms, since individual locations or functional areas may take on the character of hostile, or desirable, depending on the impact to the constituents. A frequently noted example of a friendly/hostile takeover is one driven by A. Dunlap. When A. Dunlap acquired a company, stockholders were generally pleased, while employees were generally unsettled or nervous. This, of course, could vary by function or classification of employee or by locations.

Communications should consider all constituents—on a prioritized basis—to ensure that adequate communications plans are developed. As you review the impact of an acquisition, you may find certain locations, employee groups, vendors, or even customers may have differing opinions of the acquisition. As an example, the acquisition of First Alert by Sunbeam may initially seem amicable until you consider that the headquarters staff at First Alert may be redundant and almost immediately eliminated. The headquarters staff may consider the takeover to be a hostile event. If multiple classifications (e.g., hostile/friendly) can be attributed to the acquisition, the matrix should be expanded to reflect all the major elements of the constituencies (e.g., the HQ may consider the takeover hostile, while the stockholders consider the transaction desirable).

Hostile Takeover

A hostile takeover of a company will very likely be extremely emotional. A hostile takeover means that the acquired company (i.e., the board of directors, senior management, and/or employees) does not want to be acquired, for business reasons (valuations are opportunistic for the acquirer, due to market factors), personal reasons (management believes that it is doing an excellent job and does not believe the acquirer will do as well), or perhaps job security reasons. Hostile takeovers frequently result in job losses, factory shutdowns, and downsizing for the benefit of the acquirer or the resulting company. Content, tone, and selected audiences must be carefully considered before any information is released.

A hostile takeover generates considerable negative energy and a serious dilution of productivity. During a hostile takeover, the target company management may develop negative public relations campaigns against the acquiring company. They may also focus on historical performance by the acquiring company—which may be unfavorable to the employees. Their campaign may disclose unfavorable information about senior officials of the acquiring company. In a hostile takeover, the acquirer may also develop a media program to focus on performance shortfalls at the acquired company to justify their purchase.

If the transaction is considered hostile in whole or in part, the acquiring company should develop its communication campaign anticipating the adversity and negative energy. Its communications should include the following information:

- The primary responsibility is to *describe the transaction.*
- Promote the *positive aspects of the transaction,* when possible.
- Anticipate the negative feedback and *develop proactive responses* in all communications.

If the acquisition is justified, then use selected information to support the plan publicly. Communications should be truthful and reflect accurate information about topics discussed; otherwise distrust and conflict will result. Judgment, however, is critical to determine when and how selected topics will be discussed. Unless it is certain that employees will be terminated, it is best to avoid the topic until absolutely necessary. You should, however, anticipate the question.

Although an acquisition may be hostile, there may be positive differences that can be identified during the due diligence process and can occur throughout the business. For example, perhaps the acquiring company has a strong market share, has an excellent reputation, and uses only the most advanced equipment; it requires continuous training for job enrichment; or it maintains a job posting system for career development.

Background

An example of a positive presentation is as follows:

The target company employees expect layoffs due to redundant headquarters personnel. The target company is a small, "family-oriented" organization with minimal fringe benefits but a "lot of heart." The acquiring company is a larger, well-organized company. As such, routine benefits may include 401k, tuition assistance, on-the-job training, and routine procedures such as annual reviews.

Strategy

Internal correspondence and discussion with employees should focus on the benefits of the "new organization." The communication plans will be forthright and discuss the potential for layoffs, but will also reflect additional benefits of the new organization. While this will not resolve any terminated employees' personal concerns, it will discuss the benefits of the new organization to the acquired company as a whole.

The plan anticipates the negative reactions and, if appropriate, preempts the reactions in the communication.

The acquiring company's communication process team must be extremely careful in the timing, content, and tone of all communications. The communications plan should be prepared and approved by senior management before any formal communications begin. Although the communications plan will be discussed later in this chapter, it is essential that written and verbal communications be properly crafted to ensure that the areas of major concern to the constituents have been appropriately considered.

Friendly Takeovers

Friendly takeovers often develop a different tone and are easier to manage since they generally have the endorsement of the boards, essential management, and possibly the entire workforce. Although the combined operations may still have layoffs, the tone of friendly takeovers is generally for the common good of all constituents.

A friendly takeover causes much less concern than a hostile takeover. A friendly takeover may be the result of negotiations by senior management to assure that all constituents of the acquired company have been fairly treated. This does not necessarily mean that management desires the acquisition, but rather that they are meeting their fiduciary responsibility to sell or maximize the company's value. As you broadly think through the acquisition, build a matrix of all the major constituents—include employees, stockholders, vendors, customers, and so on as in Exhibit 4.2. A very healthy, positive merger may have dissatisfied groups. Review the matrix with the integration teams to anticipate good and bad reactions, and use the matrix as one factor to develop the communications plan. Consider that the First Alert acquisition reflects management meeting their responsibility to maximize value for the shareholders, although employee terminations will most likely result.

The merger of Citicorp and Travelers Insurance Company is the result of a "friendly" consolidation, where two potential rivals reached an agreement that will have minimal impact on total employment.[18] Even friendly takeovers should be carefully reviewed to ensure that there are no significant pockets of adversity. When reviewing for such significant pockets, all constituents (vendors, stockholders, customers, competitors) should be considered.

PLANNING COMMUNICATIONS

Effective communications are an important part of the integration process. Communications represent an information pipeline that dispels misinformation and rumors and that establishes a tone of honesty and cooperation. Planning elements that are important include timing, content, and audience. The initial discussion or press release of the integration should consider the affected constituents and the expected impact. Exhibit 4.2 is an example worksheet that will assist in defining the issues.

Consider the impact upon each local community that may result from the acquisition. For example, if a small town such as Norwich, New York, were to lose 500 jobs due to company relocation, it would have a significant negative impact on the community. The company may expect reactions from local legislators, union leadership, and church and social organizations.

Hewlett-Packard has considered frequent and complete communications to be critical to the success of the integration process:

HP managers pledge to keep employees informed. HP brought the top 400 managers of the merged company to a weekend meeting in San Francisco last month. It has named three levels of managers and is in the process of naming a fourth.

Ann Livermore, head of HP's computer-services business, met with her top 150 managers, who include former Compaq employees, last week in San Francisco.

EXHIBIT 4.2 Matrix of Constituents

Build a matrix of affected people, organizations and interested parties, listing them on the left and the impact across the top of the matrix. Consider grouping the constituents, and the impact if it makes sense, to develop a more clear understanding of the communications challenge. An example worksheet follows:

Employees

Alternative 1	*Alternative 2*	*Alternative 3*	*Alternative 4*
Employees:	**Employees:**	**Employees:**	**Employees:**
- Exempt	- Atlanta	- Engineers	- Male: <30
- Non-exempt	- Poughkeepsie	- Sales	- Male: >30
- Union	- Ithaca	- Manufacturing	- Female: >30

CUSTOMERS   *RETIREES*   *COMPETITORS*

Customers: **Customers:**
- National Accounts   - Service
- Regions ($ 5 Million +) - Product:
- Northeast   - Capital
- Southeast   - Parts
- Midwest   - Upgrades
- Pacific North

WORKSHEET

					Personnel					
				Compensation			**Benefits**			
Description	**Workload**	**Employment**	**Base**	**Bonus**	**Options**	**Health Ins.**	**Life Ins.**	**Tuition**		
- Exempt										
- Non-exempt				⊙⊙⊙			⊙⊙			
- Union							◁◁			
- Temporary										
- Part-time										

LEGEND

⊙ Major

◁ Somewhat

◇ Minimal

Consider color coding, using various shapes to depict the environment that you encounter. Shapes allow you to frame an image without precise calculations, and also allow you to convey the assessment more effectively to others.

This week, Ms. Livermore will visit offices in Littleton, Mass., Atlanta, Toronto and Silicon Valley to "make sure every single employee understands their role and the focus of the business," she says. . . .

The integration planning, which HP says involved more than 1,000 employees who worked more than one million hours, drew praise even from skeptics of the deal. The detailed product plans, for one, are a big improvement over historical practice. It took Compaq more than a year after its Digital acquisition to choose which products would survive. HP also unveiled a new Web site, where users can buy former Compaq products.[19]

The communications plan should also consider the competitive environment. Remember that all public disclosures—even those company confidential releases—may be available to the competitors. Other nonconfidential conversations with employees and casual discussions with inside and outside personnel may also include information useful to competitors. In transition periods, with uneasy or insecure personnel, it is possible that information may be inadvertently released to competition. Assume that the content of all communications eventually are released to competitors, and prepare accordingly.

Planning requires that a checklist of questions be considered, as listed in Exhibit 4.3.

Planning requires that the purpose of the transaction is thoroughly understood by both parties to the transaction and that the expected impact of the transaction is defined. Timing and probable integration activity should be identified when possible. The expected impact on constituents important or critical to the business should be defined. This can be accomplished by developing a written plan outlining:

- Appointment of a communications coordinator
- Assembling a team to be responsible for all communications
- Development of an approximate communication schedule
- Identifying significantly affected constituents
- Estimating the timing of major activities and discussing the deal with the communications coordinator
- Developing an approval matrix for all "content" for communications
- Defining the approved methods of communicating with third parties (e.g., Web site, internal newsletters, and customer newsletters)

The written plan is merely a guideline and not an inflexible rule. In order to be effective, the plan should allow for changes based on prevailing conditions. While these many steps may seem excessive, the steps are merely a checklist of responsibilities. Depending on the size of the organization, the steps may be completed by one person fairly quickly. The key is to consider all the items in the plan.

EXHIBIT 4.3   Communications Questions

Questions	Guidance
WHO should be addressed?	Constituents in general, and particular audience when communicating ... the audience and media may change ...
WHAT should be disclosed?	Facts or issues that should be described at this time. These can be generated in part from the matrix of issues and concerns.
WHEN should we communicate?	As soon as practical, considering the integration strategy.
WHERE will the message be delivered?	Target a specific audience, but assume that the world (including your competitors...) will see the information.
HOW will the information be released?	Verbal/written ... Media: Print, Video, Audio, Focus Groups, Town Meetings etc. The media used should reflect the intended message. If there is no intent to field questions, written material, or video may be the best solution.

The communications plan should include a mix of *written as well as verbal discussions*. In all cases, designated individuals at each location and for each company must review the information before release or discussion with the employees. An approval checklist should be prepared to ensure that only approved communications have been released. One certain method to cover all possible formal communications is to use the finance or legal function as the "gatekeeper" since, in many mergers, these functions are responsible for public information—in compliance with the SEC's and other agency's regulations. The checklist should define an officer to be responsible for the communications at each company—the acquirer and the acquired. The gatekeeper should ensure that all the required functions have reviewed the correspondence before release of the information. This doesn't necessarily mean all functions must review every piece of correspondence, but those directly affected by the communications should be aware of the information before release. See Exhibit 4.4 for an example.

In the plan, each of the constituent groups should be considered. Timing and content should be discussed whenever possible. It is essential that each communication be as forthright and honest as possible. *Ineffective communication could result in a failed acquisition.*

It is best to avoid speculation and rumors by presenting the facts for review. Companies such as General Electric and Cisco that have successfully integrated acquisition have found that forthright communications ultimately made the integration more successful. Whenever possible, a timetable of activity should be included with the communication to demonstrate accountability and control over the merger and acquisition

EXHIBIT 4.4 Communications Plan Review

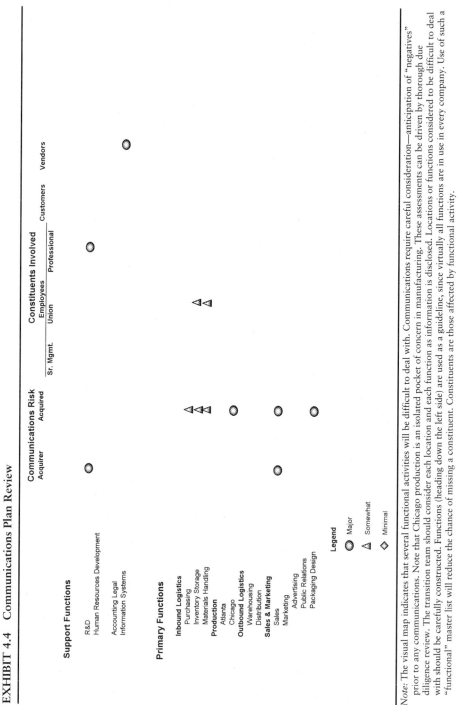

Note: The visual map indicates that several functional activities will be difficult to deal with. Communications require careful consideration—anticipation of "negatives" prior to any communications. Note that Chicago production is an isolated pocket of concern in manufacturing. These assessments can be driven by thorough due diligence review. The transition team should consider each location and each function as information is disclosed. Locations or functions considered to be difficult to deal with should be carefully constructed. Functions (heading down the left side) are used as a guideline, since virtually all functions are in use in every company. Use of such a "functional" master list will reduce the chance of missing a constituent. Constituents are those affected by functional activity.

process. If it is likely that employee termination or plant closure will result, it is important that these be carefully discussed before any release to the employees. Wherever possible, terminations should be completed as fairly as possible to avoid reactions from other employees.

Plan Content

The first part of the communication process is to define the transaction including expected results, pricing, timing of expected changes, and purpose of the transaction. This requires careful crafting, since the information may be useful to your competitors. In 2001, Hewlett-Packard announced a friendly merger with Compaq Computer. Unfortunately, due to some misalignment in the Hewlett-Packard executive offices, a board member publicly opposed the merger. This was clearly a poorly executed segment of the communications plan developed by Carly Fiorina and the transition team. During the next several months, the PC market became disrupted, and competitors such as Dell Computer and Gateway watched the confusion enhance their business. The purpose of the transaction was the foundation of the communication theme to build upon throughout the transition process. Hewlett-Packard's intent may be to extend its critical mass in PCs, expand its product line to include servers, and improve service. HP's theme may be to improve shareholder value through better customer service and broader product lines, and improve employee welfare through training and expanded opportunity within a larger growing organization. These themes address shareholders, customers, and employees. As a plan is developed, the theme should be continually reinforced throughout the integration process. HP has invested considerable effort in communicating with all constituents.

Note in Exhibit 4.5 of the Citicorp and Travelers merger that the approximate timing and broad purpose have been effectively defined.

Note how Citicorp and Travelers are complementary and that the combination may result in little employee turnover based on the lack of duplication of product and services within the businesses. The summary described reflects the words used by the two CEOs to outline their intended strategy in their public discussions about the merger.

The plan should be *written and provide for both outbound and inbound communications (feedback),* and it should consider the constituents of both the acquirer and the acquired organizations. Remember that the acquirer may also suffer from disrupted operations due to the extensive workload and possible reduction of force. During the transition period, communication should be scheduled at established frequencies to ensure that everyone is well informed about activities completed and in process, and to ensure that the momentum of the transition is maintained. If there is a large gap in communications, people may assume something is wrong, and the rumor mill will potentially guide the transaction to an unfavorable

EXHIBIT 4.5   Synergies of Citicorp/Travelers Merger

Business segments	Citibank	Travelers
Credit card	7	—
Investment services	4	22
Insurance	—	14
Retail	6	—
All other	5	2
Total	22	38

Source: Business Week, April 20, 1998, 38.

Excerpts of the Citigroup press release follow:

> The combination will bring together two organizations with core commitments to serving consumers, corporations, institutions, and governments globally, through a diverse array of sales and service channels. The merged company's principal thrusts will be traditional banking, consumer finance, credit cards, investment banking, securities brokerage and asset management, and property casualty and life insurance. . . .
>
> The combined company, which will be named Citigroup Inc. . . .
>
> Serving as Co-Chairman and Co-Chief Executive Officers of Citigroup. . . .
>
> We are committed to maintaining the unique mix of businesses this merger creates. . . .
>
> Each company's shareholders will own 50% of the combined enterprise. The agreement calls for Citicorp shareholders to exchange each of their shares for 2.5 shares of Citigroup in a tax-free exchange. . . .
>
> The companies expect to generate substantial incremental earnings from the significant cross-selling opportunities that will be created as well as cost savings that will be realized.

Notes:

1. The company has recognized the value of customers in the press release. This also indicates the value chain analysis: sales and marketing delivery to the customers, leverage using existing forces. The broad company products and customers have been highlighted.
2. Serving as Co-Chairman defines the leadership roles to be served by the executives.
3. Commitments to constituents such as customers, vendors, and possibly employees, stating that the diverse mix of products will continue.
4. Pricing and method of payment has been effectively disclosed.
5. Business process focuses on the "cross-selling" as the main theme of the merger. There may also be some cost savings, but these are ancillary benefits. The theme is one of "blending two companies," which the *Business Week* article adequately describes. See Citicorp/Citibank, "Citicorp and Travelers group to merge, creating Citicorp: The global leader in financial services," press release, April 6, 1998.

result. A feedback process should be outlined in the communications plan to be sure that the team listens to the participants. An early warning about problems can help resolve the problem as well as improve communications. The feedback process will provide insight into how the transaction is viewed—at both the acquired and the acquiring organization.

As you review hostile versus friendly, consider how the communication may change if the transaction is hostile. The transaction should be reviewed from all constituents' viewpoints (such as employees, stockholders, customers, vendors, analysts, and government agencies) to anticipate questions and reactions to the acquisition announcement.

Communications Coordinator (Concentrate the Energy)

The communications coordinator should be experienced in communication with the press and major constituents such as stockholders, board members, and employees. The coordinator should have a good understanding about how decisions will affect the groups, and the possible reactions to changes that may result. The coordinator should be able to anticipate the constituents' reactions and prepare controlled responses to items that are major issues—for example, plant closures; discontinued product lines; and layoffs. The coordinator should be sure that processes are established to capture feedback from the major constituents. The feedback should be summarized periodically and reviewed with the integration team and senior management.

An officer—either the officer in charge of the integration transaction or the chief operating officer—should be one of the checkpoints of approval for outside communications. This will avoid communication problems, such as erroneous information being released or information being released at an inappropriate time.

If communications are not well managed, the management process will lose credibility and the successful integration process may be jeopardized.

Each business should identify the communications coordinator using both the official and the informal organization chart. Companies often have an informal chain of command that should be understood prior to establishing the communication process. Opinion leaders as well as formal leaders in each organization should understand the content before the formal communications begin. These preliminary communications reviews can occur in meetings, e-mail, or telephone discussions.

Communications Teams

The coordinator should assemble a communications review team consisting of personnel from both organizations. A cross-functional team may provide the broadest outbound communication, but cross-functional will also ensure a better understanding of the reaction from the constituents.

The purpose of the team is to plan and execute the communications to effectively discuss the transaction, transition plans, and periodic status reports. Team members will also be one source of feedback from the constituents. Remember, the purpose of the team is to ensure two-way communications throughout the integration process. When appropriate, team members will lead meetings at key locations; and questions will be answered both formally and informally.

Define Constituents

The value chain of all functions within both organizations will be one basis of the review to determine significant constituents, since it represents all activities of the firm. All components of the value chain should be considered—that is, any significant operation, location, function, or group of activities. Don't forget the challenges of international operations due to the social and legal requirements of many countries/regions (e.g., France, Germany, Scandinavia, Japan, and Latin America). You may want to hire local experts (e.g., local representatives of CPA firms, major consulting companies, or law firms) to review the transaction implications on each international location.

Locations can also be listed and assessed to identify the expected difficulty to communicate with the employees.

The team members should identify the constituents to ensure that all significantly affected people, organizations, and communities have been properly considered in the transition and communications process. Use a team to ensure that the broadest possible definition of constituent is used in the analysis. As with many of the transition areas, judgment is an essential element of the definition, especially as it relates to the definition of "significant." Both business operations—the buyer and the target company—should be considered when defining constituents, since both organizations may be affected. The definition of constituent should also consider information obtained by the due diligence team—the first line of information for the integration process. Each element or point of information represents an opportunity for success or failure in the integration process.

Transition Planning

Another key element of the communications process is the timing of the integration process itself. The integration team leader should schedule and coordinate major activities for the entire acquisition/integration process. These may be initially just "blocked time frames" such as "Move Distribution Center—second quarter," or a more precise timetable such as "Move Distribution Center May 3–10." Broad timing may be adequate for the initial communication planning, but planning should always consider the next steps. As the transition process is reviewed, the communication schedule should also be blocked to reflect planned activities. Plans may not always proceed as scheduled, but broad guidelines will allow for sequencing of events and contingency plans if necessary.

Approval Matrix

An approval matrix should be developed for all formal and scheduled informal communication during the transition. The matrix should identify an individual who is personally responsible for reviewing the timing, content, and proper release of the information. For example, the vice president of manufacturing must review and approve all releases that relate to manufacturing operations, sites, and employees. The coordinator will complete the final coordination of the releases.

DEFINE CONSTITUENTS WITH MAJOR IMPACT

Each constituent may have a reaction—either positive or negative—to an acquisition. Significant positive and negative reactions should be anticipated and scripted based on senior management's expectations. High-low probabilities should be assigned to these reactions to anticipate questions from the audience. When an acquisition announcement is made, each constituent group will ask: "What impact will this have on *me*?" Consider the impact of the HP-Compaq merger. Certainly employees expressed personal concern about the merger, but the merger may affect major customers and vendors around the globe as well as whole communities.

Employees

Generally, employees will be concerned for their future security. This could include everything from continued employment and benefits to vesting rights in existing programs such as 401k's and pension plans. They will also be concerned about operating style, rules, and organization structure—even the simplest culture changes.

Employees may also be concerned about relative compensation levels and benefits, which will be discussed in more detail later. If possible, the acquiring company should avoid discussing specifics about compensation, benefits, and so on in any public document early in the transaction. Generally, unless the companies have made the decisions based on a thorough analysis, just state the facts: "We are reviewing the organizations and have not yet formalized." The success or failure of the merger rests heavily on the credibility of the management team's actions and communication process.

If communication is absolutely necessary, limit the communication to broad statements about future employment to reduce mistrust and misunderstanding. The statements should be based on short- and long-term plans, and should address employee concerns. However, these statements must be truthful. That is, the company should not state that there would be no job losses if losses were reasonably possible within the merged organization. General statements such as "We intend to maintain employment in the Chicago location to ensure our continued . . ." may be useful to describe the intent without making a firm commitment to the employees. If restructuring is required, state it. Employees are very perceptive and will not tolerate misrepresentations and lies.

Stockholders

Stockholders generally have a primary investment goal—to increase the value of their investments. Value does not necessarily mean the investment in a particular company but overall wealth. As such, stockholders will approve an acquisition transaction on a financial basis only if they believe the present value of the offer exceeds the present value of the expected stock growth while the target company management is in place. In unfriendly takeovers, the lack of endorsement by management is saying one of two things:

- Management will improve the value of your investment more than the offered price.
- Management may also be saying that it wants continued employment, and the status quo is the only certain assurance of this.

In the Compaq–Hewlett-Packard merger, Walter Hewlett made a clear case that value would be reduced in a merged organization. This public disagreement most certainly strained the smooth integration of the two major companies. In a friendly takeover, when viewed as a purely financial decision, management has considered the discounted present value of the expected earnings flow without a takeover versus with, and it considers the offer best for the stockholders. Management may also often consider the affected employees. Stockholder composition by type of investor may impact the acceptance of a merger. Venture capitalists and institutional holders may be more likely to sell for an immediate, certain profit rather than wait for management to perform. Widely held stocks—perhaps with less sophisticated investors or perhaps individual investors—may view the acquisition with more concern for the employees and therefore have less urgency to sell.

Analysts and Wall Street

Analysts are often viewed as "short-term oriented." It is therefore difficult for analysts to vote against premiums of 30 to 50 percent over the current value, although they are not privy to the information available to the selling management or board of directors. Unfortunately, analysts and major investors may often approve the sale of the company due to the short-term profits that can be realized from the sale.

Customers

During the past decade, long-term relationships with customers have become more like partnerships due to a focus by many companies on the value chain. Customers, in effect, may have delegated part of their supply chain responsibility to companies in exchange for long-term, formal, or informal supply commitments to the companies. During a hostile takeover, customers that have such partnering relationships with companies may become concerned. Communications with these important customers must reflect the proper tone and include pertinent information to avoid unnecessary disruption of the relationship. In the HP deal, the employee in charge of Europe, the Middle East, and Africa has focused attention on communicating with key customers.

Two weeks prior to launch (this week) we had named and selected more than 140 senior managers across EMEA. All of these people, including myself, are now calling our 150 largest customers and explaining to them what this company is about and what our product road maps are. We have also assigned a customer-engagement manager and customer-business manager to each of them.[20]

Good customer relationships must be maintained throughout the negotiation, acquisition, and integration process. In a hostile takeover, the negotiation process must be brief to avoid alienating customers or losing customers to competitors (e.g., PricewaterhouseCoopers losing customers to Deloitte & Touche during Price Waterhouse and Coopers & Lybrand's merger). Although it may be unlikely in a hostile takeover, the target company management may consider working with the acquirer to reinforce the continued business relationships with the customers to protect the core employee base. The acquirer should be prepared to address customer concerns as soon as possible.

Conversely, in a friendly takeover, the senior management of the acquired company will immediately endorse the takeover, and should assure customers of continued supply arrangements. It is also possible that customers are common to both the target and acquirer. The sentiment of hostile/friendly takeover, considering all constituents, must be reflected in any communications plan.

During the HP-Compaq merger, one of the first activities was to formally establish the product offering.

She [Carly Fiorina] and Mr. Capellas, now HP's president, said they are ahead of their schedule in integrating the two companies. They outlined three-year plans for every product, and named sales teams for the company's 100 biggest customers.

HP said it will continue to sell personal computers to consumers under both the HP and Compaq brands, but will use only the Compaq label for business-oriented PCs. The company will use HP as the overall brand for the back-end computers called servers, though some old Compaq brands will live on as server model names.[21]

Vendors

Vendors suffer with similar emotions, as do customers in any takeover. Vendors effectively form these "partner" relationships with companies and potentially suffer a business risk if there are no formal agreements. Important vendors may require the same type of assurance as major customers to avoid supply disruptions.

Government Agencies

Government agencies are important to consider in acquisition transactions. For example, the U.S. Department of Justice must be satisfied that it does not violate the Hart-Scott-Rodino Antitrust Improvements Act, but the impact of other agencies that are integral to the success of the business should be considered in any communications plan. Government agencies may also be involved in negotiations related to potential infractions of EPA laws, tax laws, and other legal matters. For example, product approvals and new product development process applications may be pending at the FDA. The team leader must consider existing and potential relationships (because of the acquisition) and develop a communications plan to deal with these constituents appropriately.

MAJOR ACTIVITIES

The communications plan should be based on expected major activities. As a merger proceeds, certain activities can be reasonably predicted. For example, the government response timetable related to the Hart-Scott-Rodino Act is defined. Often, companies have specific timetables that they traditionally adhere to when completing an acquisition. For example, companies such as General Electric and Cisco may use a 100-day plan for many of their acquisitions. Major activities can include data systems mergers, sales force combinations, catalog changes, advertising changes, personnel and benefits changes, and vendor and customer account consolidations.

All elements of the value chain should be considered in the integration timing. See Exhibit 4.6, which provides a graphic display of major activities, constituents involved, and approximate timing. Once major activities are mapped, management can view the timing and probability of positive and negative comments, and structure the communications plan to more effectively manage the constituents. A plant closure, for

EXHIBIT 4.6 Communications Planning: Content

Description	Responsibility	Priority	Probability %	January (week) 1	2	3	4	February (week) 1	2	3	4
Announce Acquisition		A	90		$$$$						
Plant Closures											
Chicago	Manufacturing - c	C	50					$$			
Atlanta	Manufacturing - a	A	80						$$$		
Facilities Expansion											
New Sales Offices											
Houston		C	50								
Charleston		C	50								
Seattle		C	50								
International Expansion											
Acquire Japan Dealer			90								
Acquire Mexico Dealer			20								

The chart includes many points of information. The objective is to understand the overall communications process, and the numerous messages that are expected in the near future. In this case, the "$" is used to indicate the magnitude of the announcement - more dollar signs are more significant. Probability is the likelihood of the activity actually occurring, and the timing which becomes less precise as we look out further into the future. A similar presentation will provide a balanced communication to all the constituents. International Expansion represents activities unrelated to the acquisition & its integration, but scheduled in the normal course of business.

example, may disclose the minimal amount of information related to the closure. Additional releases, which present a fair balance of information, may also disclose a positive event, like enhancement of the pension plan. The communications plan should not be manipulative but rather should present the balanced picture of the acquisition. The timing of major events will trigger actions in the communication schedule. Events that are negative should be coordinated with positive activity when possible—for example, a plant closing should be announced with major product launches. Again, sensitivity to events, actions, and constituents is critical.

PUBLIC AND PRIVATE COMPANY TRANSACTIONS

As companies develop a communications plan for a public company transaction, it is important to properly and legally inform the analysts and Wall Street investors about expectations of the transaction. As public acquisitions occur, the acquirer must legally disclose the "purpose of the tender offer and plans or proposals of the bidder," according to the Securities Exchange Act of 1934:

State the purpose or purposes of the tender offer. . . . Describe any plans or proposals that relate to or would result in:
1. An extraordinary corporate transaction, such as a merger, reorganization, or liquidation involving the subject company or any of its subsidiaries;
2. A sale or transfer of a material amount of assets of the subject company or any of its subsidiaries;
3. Any change in the present board of directors or management of the subject company;
4. Any material change in the present capitalization or dividend policy of the subject company;
5. Any other material change in the Subject Company's corporate structure or business.[22]

Private company disclosures are generally contractually oriented. Communication may be required to secured debtors, banks, and unions (if represented), and for other contractual obligations such as licensing agreements for patents, trademarks, copyrights, and the like.

Once the major terms of the letter of intent have been resolved, disclosure is legally required. Acquisitions of private companies by publicly traded companies need disclosure only if the acquisition represents a material transaction to the acquirer. However, financial institutions involved with either private or public companies may find that an acquisition has a dramatic impact on their business portfolio. Communication requirements and possibly approvals will be outlined in the financing documents negotiated by the parties.

As communication plans are developed, legal requirements—statutory or contractual—should be carefully reviewed. Loan agreements and contracts that exist but are not public may define both private and public company requirements. In addition to the SEC requirements, representing attorneys should be familiar with terms of significant contracts to ensure that there is adequate disclosure.

All public disclosures should reflect concern about forward-looking statements as defined by the SEC. Certain legal benefits can be maintained by establishing a specific disclaimer related to specific forward-looking statements. An example of such a broad disclaimer is as follows:

Except for the historical information contained herein, this news release contains forward-looking statements regarding the appeal of new products and the gaining of new customers. The risks and uncertainties associated with the continued acceptance of the new products, competition market growth, and timely availability and the pricing of products, as well as other risks detailed in the company's SEC reports, could cause actual results to differ from those in the forward-looking statements.

Acquisitions in the international environment add complexity. Again, securities laws and public disclosure laws in each country may vary. As in prior chapters, it is *strongly recommended that an acquirer engage international firms—Big Five CPA firms or international legal advisers—to ensure that all significant disclosure requirements have been properly completed.*

OTHER THIRD-PARTY COMMUNICATIONS

An essential element to a successful transition is the effective change in all product literature, sales information, audio/video material, product commercials, product packaging, and internal communications. Once all materials have been assembled, representatives should review the materials in relation to the transaction and accept or schedule to modify them as required on a prioritized basis. Ideally, the review should be a cooperative effort by both companies and should consider the legal, sales, marketing, and emotional issues involved in the acquisition. Again, the type of transaction and the purpose of the transaction may drive urgency. If the takeover is hostile, it is best to move through the communications swiftly to avoid dilution of the newly created image.

On a prioritized basis, all forms of fixed media communications should be reviewed to determine, based on the type of transaction and the ultimate goal of the consolidation, the required action. The purpose of the transaction may also drive the urgency of the transition and the revision of published material. Marketing-driven acquisitions may require an accelerated review and revision to newly approved materials. International acquisitions represent considerably more business risk and should be thoroughly reviewed to effectively prepare a communications plan. The nuances of each country's culture may affect how the transactions are presented to the constituents. As a result, specialists in communications for each country should be consulted if it appears to be a challenging integration process. All organizations should carefully consider the implication of international acquisitions. The communications should consider internal and external communications such as policy manuals, product instruction manuals, advertising materials, and packaging. Stationery, blank checks, business cards, and other forms of representation should be reviewed to determine if immediate replacement is required. The reviewers from all functions are responsible to understand the impact of the media communications and the urgency for revision. Each functional head must examine the material and consider the impact of not changing the communications. The functional representative should document and assemble all materials that require revision. The most effective method to ensure a complete review is to require a formal sign-off by responsible personnel that all communications have been properly reviewed.

The communications coordinators for each functional area should prepare master schedules of all documents, including print and commercial media, to be sure that the review has been properly completed. However, the main task is to advise the functional representatives that they have the primary responsibility for identifying all third-party communications that require modifications.

QUICK CHECK OF CHAPTER 4

✓ Type of takeover: hostile or friendly
✓ Communications plan—constituents
✓ Managing the plan
✓ Who is addressed?
✓ What to communicate?
✓ When to communicate?
✓ Where to communicate?
✓ How to communicate?
✓ Key elements of the plan

5

Employees, Culture, and Other Factors That Affect Integration

In virtually all acquisitions, satisfactory relationships with employees in *both the acquiring and target companies* are essential to a smooth transition. It is particularly difficult to be successful if one group of employees becomes alienated and opposes a smooth transition. Personal concerns about job security, loss of fringe benefits, changed procedures, loss of corporate or personal identity, and overall culture change may be the foundation for alienation of an employee group.

In general, plans developed using the formal and informal leadership in each organization will assist in a smoother transition. The receptiveness to the merger may vary dramatically based on the type of transaction. Let's continue to define a hostile takeover as one not endorsed by the target company management and company employees. Some transactions that may appear to be friendly since they are endorsed by the stockholders and major investors may actually be antagonistic or hostile to the employees. For planning purposes, these should be considered hostile takeovers and managed as such.

Much of the impact on individual employees—if they are retained in the merged organization—will result from changes in procedures, process, and culture. It is possible for employees to oppose change or to appear to be adapting to change while not really supporting the transition. It is important to establish a baseline for both organizations to determine the extent of damage control that may be necessary if the transaction is not embraced. Members of the due diligence team and the transition team should review documents such as organization charts and policy and procedure manuals that establish the basis of the culture. During the due diligence review, the reviewer should observe employee actions, since the actions will provide insight into the undocumented processes and organization.

It is important to understand that either a hostile or a friendly acquisition may have a *dramatic impact on both the acquirer and the acquired company.* Ideally, the buyer will ensure that the due diligence review team includes at least some members of the transition team. This is very important, due to the linkage of the due diligence and planning teams, and knowledge may be lost if there is not a transfer of knowledge from the due diligence team.

Again, planning is critical. Employee transition planning includes defining the baseline, understanding the type of transaction, identifying short- and long-term goals for the organizations, and identifying key employees. As these goals are defined, transition plans—reviewed and approved by senior management or the executive responsible for the transaction—are essential. This chapter will discuss reviewing all the functions and locations in the entire organization. This review should reflect the leader's judgment about priority areas, based on input from the due diligence team, knowledge of the transaction, and discussion with key constituents. The leader may decide that, for example, the Boise, Idaho, sales office may not be reviewed, since it is not a critical variable in the transition or integration process.

The valuation and purchase strategy should define the strategy or theme of the acquisition. For example, the theme of the acquisition may be to focus on consolidating operations for distribution and sales, consolidate product development, or perhaps expand distribution of the acquiring company's product line. Examples of other themes would be consolidation of a fragmented industry, expansion of market share or geographic reach, or acquisition of critical resources (people or tangible property such as natural resources). Remember that during the due diligence process and negotiation, the company is not yet acquired. As such, any disruption in the target company's HR function may result in a lawsuit or collapse of the negotiation.

TRANSACTION TYPE

The type of transaction—hostile or friendly—will have a major impact on the receptiveness by employees. The initial designation of transaction type is straightforward: *hostile* means not endorsed by management, whereas *friendly* means endorsed by management. However, a subset of the friendly takeover may exist. As an example, the employees may not agree with the management acceptance of a proposed merger due to its impact on personal financial security. In the Hewlett-Packard and Compaq merger, the transaction was a friendly merger at the senior management and board level, but at the employee levels it may have been viewed as hostile, because up to 15,000 employees were terminated. The challenge for HP has been further complicated by the culture change that has been in process within HP.

As Ms. Fiorina seeks to meld the HP and Compaq cultures, she will certainly draw on recent experience. When she arrived at HP, she faced "the HP Way," the almost-sacrosanct culture of founders David Packard and Bill Hewlett. She said the culture had become a "gentle bureaucracy of entitlement and consensus," and she sought to bring it back to its roots of valuing the individual, rewarding creativity and focusing on great engineering.

Compaq and HP have long been fiercely competitive rivals, and several analysts brought up the point that it may be hard to get the employees to switch gears and accept each other with open arms. Blending two huge organizations—Compaq has 62,000 workers and HP has 87,000—isn't an insignificant part of making the acquisition work. Ms. Fiorina maintained that the melding of the two cultures would go smoothly, because there are many parallels between them.[23]

Once the issues have been identified, the management team can develop solutions to employee concerns. Employee continuity is often a critical element of a successful integration; if employees leave the company, the merger becomes more expensive as replacements are hired and trained, and the merger's success is jeopardized. It is important to understand that in a successful transition, the employees of the resulting organization must work together. Management at each organization must understand that the only method to ensure that the venture will succeed is to ensure cooperation among the employees. Early in the due diligence process, the team must search for and identify real or potential discontent, points of dissatisfaction, and points of conflict that may result from the acquisition. Assessment of personnel and their acceptance of the merger are critical elements of any merger transaction.

Historically, employee turnover has often been the result of a company acquisition. In a 1986 study by H. Unger, he noted that senior executive turnover reached almost 50 percent in the first year, rising to nearly 75 percent within 3 years.[24]

EMPLOYEES

Employees: Buyer/Target Company

As the target company is identified, the buyer should understand that both companies might be affected by the acquisition. "Buyer" employees may be pleased with the acquisition, due to the potential for expanded responsibility and career growth. However, employees may also be threatened by the potential impact on their workload or job security. How often have we seen an acquisition justified by stated synergies, which may eliminate resources but not effectively reduce the workload? Employee insecurity is not only limited to the target company employees. The professionalism and competence of the target company may also threaten buyer company employees. This type of insight is important to understand before the transaction is completed and can be identified by having highly qualified personnel participating in the due diligence and transition planning tasks. Team members and leaders should be vigilant to identify insecurity or undue concern in the ranks of both companies.

Hewlett-Packard has focused on these critical needs, and Carly Fiorina has stated:

> Employee communication is as vital right now as shareowner communication, and it takes many forms. First, we have asked our senior management team to be proactive in communicating with employees on a constant basis. Secondly, I personally have engaged in a lot of employee communication, whether that is meeting with groups of employees around the country and the world, or Webcasting meetings.
>
> We don't guess at employee morale, we survey it. HP has used employee surveys pretty systematically for many years. I continued that process, because it makes a lot of sense. I think surveys are particularly important when you dealing with change, because change can create powerful emotions.[25]

The target company employees may feel the same emotions but on a much broader scale, since they do not know the buyer company's management style. Target company employees will often be reluctant to sell the company due to fear of an unknown future environment. Target company employees will consider the buyer's reputation established in previous merger transactions as a reflection of their view of the pending transaction.

As potential deals are defined, it is important to consider the personal impact on each company's employees. *The review should consider all levels, all locations, and all types of employees* (permanent, part time, and contract). For example, when Al Dunlap announced the acquisition of First Alert, based on his historical performance, the target company expected Dunlap to downsize the manufacturing operations at First Alert and shift production to the underutilized Sunbeam factory. The impact was that First Alert employees would be against the transaction and perhaps even sabotage the deal when possible. It is reasonable to think that those Sunbeam factory engineers and personnel would be in favor of the acquisition to protect their financial security. These macro factors should be considered during the review and development of transition plans.

Initial organizational or cultural goals should be confirmed, or new goals should be established, during the preliminary due diligence review, then finalized as the transaction closing approaches. In a friendly takeover, it is important that the broad plans be discussed openly *with key executives* of the target company to insure that there are no serious misinterpretations. Hostile takeovers allow little space for interaction with employees.

In friendly mergers, as specific organizational goals are identified, the goals should be reviewed with the target company to ensure that its opinion has been reasonably considered. Once the broad guidelines are established, they should be documented to form a basis of integration and possibly should be disclosed to the key employees in the target company after the acquisition has been completed. The communication should be coordinated as discussed in Chapter 4.

The preliminary plans should document the goal of the acquisition— remember that in Chapter 3 we defined "why" the purchase was made. All communications personnel in the proposed organization should be familiar with and fully support the long-range goal. As plans are being developed, the theme or strategic goal of the acquisition should be consistently reinforced. The organization charts should be prepared and reviewed with executives to ensure that the organization and functional responsibilities meet the strategic goals. The review team should review all existing locations as well as expected future changes based on the consolidated/integrated company.

Key Employees

Identify Key Employees

One of the first tasks in the organization plan is to identify the key employees who will be retained. Selection criteria to identify these employees will include:

- Critical skills and specialized training needed: "This woman has forgotten much more about micro technology than our guys ever learned" or "We're buying the company because of their service business—he runs the function with straight A's."
- Performance/Personnel education and evaluation, key company accomplishments: "One of the best manufacturing exes I've ever seen."
- Critical projects/activities and product lines: "Those data servers are the key to the success of the acquisition. Guard those folks with your life."
- Critical relationships: "For the past three years we've tried unsuccessfully to establish a European operation. We now have a foothold."

If key employees are identified in the initial definition of purpose or goal of the acquisition (e.g., R&D employees), the due diligence team should *validate the reason for the acquisition.* The due diligence review team should validate the accomplishments, capabilities, or whatever unique reasons that the company defined as a basis to acquire and value the target company in the initial purchase proposal.

During any review, it is important to understand why the business functions well, to determine if it is a formal or informal organization, and to determine if the benefit is sustainable, transferable, or has different qualities.

During the review, it may become evident that individual employees are the heart of the performance.

Key employees should be identified and/or validated by the review team. Reviewing essential processes and understanding how they are completed can be the basis of this evaluation. Reviewers will find trends that focus on the accomplishments of individuals or perhaps on groups of people in the target company. As significant accomplishments or skills are identified, the reviewer should notify the team HR representative, the functional leader, and the due diligence team leader. The unique features of the employees should be characterized, identifying factors such as leadership skills, technical skills, and customer or vendor contacts. Each factor will be helpful in assessing the employee's value to the merged organization. It is the responsibility of each executive in the due diligence team to review the organization chart for their respective functions and meet with people considered to be "key employees" to determine if the designation is true.

Retention

Key employee retention is a factor that should be considered *for both the buying company and the target company.* Key employee retention starts with the due diligence process and continues through completion of the acquisition and the initial transition period. Key employee retention is initially based on an assessment of the type of transaction (e.g., acquisition for R&D personnel, sales personnel, and/or patents), a thorough review of the value chain, and the company organization charts, if available. If key personnel are the justification for the acquisition, it is essential that these people be retained.

Plans related to key employees' continued service should be discussed with and fully coordinated with the human resources representatives on the team. If appropriate, the company should consider providing golden handcuffs or a retention bonus to hold these valuable people. The HR department should coordinate and assess the financial incentives for all golden handcuffs that will be required to retain the employee. Set up a process early in the transaction to ensure that these people know that they are important to the future of the combined company. The HR representatives should be familiar with the industry norms—for example, if biotech retention bonuses are in the 1–2-year salary range, you shouldn't offer employees six months. In all cases, key employees should be reviewed with the executive responsible for the integration of the acquisition.

The human resources representatives should also carefully coordinate any such retention discussions with the target company management. This is very important since many acquisition transactions are not completed, and the impact of poorly coordinated employee incentives may impact ongoing relationships in a failed transaction. *There should be no direct correspondence with the employees unless it is reviewed in advance with responsible target company executives.*

Golden handcuffs can take many forms, such as retention bonuses (cash), stock options, or other perquisites that may be important to the executive—such as expense allowances, vacations/sabbaticals, and club memberships. Although you shouldn't be reluctant to be creative, incentives should be determined based on industry and regional norms, which may be obtained from industry organizations, public accounting or legal firms, or surveys completed by such organizations as The Hayes Group. The cost of the incentives should be balanced with the needs of the company and the benefits expected by retaining the individual.

Industry and regional standards should be carefully considered for two reasons:

- You want to retain the employees with a fair and supportable offer.
- You should assume that extreme offers would eventually be disclosed, requiring justification to others.

For example, retention bonuses in San Francisco may be larger than in Dallas, due to the shortage of systems analysts and computer programmers, and the critical need for them in the new high-tech start-ups. Retention bonuses in high-tech areas are not unusual.

DOWNSIZING

Downsizing, rightsizing, or RIFs (reduction in force) may be necessary to trim the work force to an optimum level to meet the merger objectives. It is important that this be done fairly and equitably. Downsizing should always be coordinated with the target company's representatives—human resources, subsidiary, and functional management as appropriate. Although preliminary discussions based on valuation models and due diligence may occur before the acquisition is completed, actions must not be taken until after the company is acquired. Remember that without the support of the workforce and especially without enthusiastic cooperation of essential employees, the company's strategic goals will not be achieved.

As with any staff reductions, it is important to consult with legal counsel to be sure that applicable legislation, union contracts, or personal contracts have been properly considered. You may want to consider noncompetitive agreements for selected employees, although the enforcement of the agreements may be challenged.

As the new organization is being defined and the incentives and downsizing are being determined, you should estimate the cost and timing of these transactions. This is necessary, since part of the cost may be capitalized in the purchase price of the organization or written off as one-time charges, rather than as affecting future earnings. As the plan is developed, it is important that each senior manager be held personally responsible for the functional area review and for the plan completion. The overall plan for the transition related to employees should be reviewed and approved by senior management through the board of directors level if costs or the potential impact is material.

Opinion Leaders

Opinion leaders should be identified in the *critical process areas* that justify the acquisition. For example, if a company is being purchased for its R&D development process, the R&D development area will be a key function in which to identify opinion leaders. Other areas, such as manufacturing and sales, may not require as much attention. Be sure to focus your energy on critical areas so that you don't dilute your effectiveness.

Target Company

During the due diligence process, it is important to identify not only the opinion leaders but also the sentiment toward the transaction that may exist in the acquired company. Depending on the type of acquisition—from hostile to friendly—these opinion leaders and the overall sentiment of the employees of the acquired company are important to the successful integration of the company. The due diligence review team members should identify these opinion leaders as a required review task. A thorough and careful analysis of the organization chart to ensure that "all" people have been considered is the best way to manage the review. Remember that it is not necessarily true that the organizationally responsible managers are the ones that actually lead the company. Each level of the chart in each functional area should be considered to ensure that there are no oversights.

As opinion leaders are identified, the acquiring company representatives may work with them as an informal reference or opinion source discussing potential changes. Proceed carefully, however, since the target employees may oppose the transaction and therefore develop a negative tone about the acquisition. If these opinion leaders oppose the elements of the integration, consider the impact on the transaction's success. Observe the daily activities, and ask open-ended questions about the operations to identify opinion leaders. Observations, and not just questions and answers, should be summarized carefully by each team member and periodically reviewed with other team members to be sure that the integration team is aware of critical information.

Buyer

Identifying opinion leaders in the acquiring company is also important, since these leaders will ease the integration process if managed effectively. In some acquisitions, the target company management may be much better leaders than the acquiring company. Strong leadership in areas of the target company may present a threat to the investigators on the due diligence team. It is important that the team leader insure that there are no inconsistencies about people, processes, or activities at the target company. The team leader must carefully monitor the due diligence process. Should any misperceptions arise, it is the team leader's responsibility to ensure that they are effectively managed.

During the review, it is important to discuss preliminary goals related to employees and possible disruptions in the business itself with opinion leaders and key executives at the target company. During these discussions, two important criteria must be considered:

- Discussions must remain confidential and not be disclosed to the entire organization. This becomes particularly difficult when the reviewer is not familiar with the company "grapevine."
- Conversations must be open and candid to insure that the relevant information is being assessed.

CULTURE

Employee turnover is a significant cost in the first few years of any integration project. Keith Symmers, vice president at Best Practices LLC, has estimated that, "47% of top managers at acquired companies leave within three years."[26]

In major acquisitions, such as when Chase Manhattan bought J. P. Morgan, the culture clash was exceptional and permeated the entire organization. The cultures of old line, conservative banking at J. P. Morgan clashed with the brash young upstarts at Chase.

When Chase bought J. P. Morgan in late 2000, for $33 billion, Wall Street buzzed over the yawning upstairs/downstairs gulf in cultures—the prospect of flying plates when the cerebral, upper-crust bankers from the House of Morgan shared the table with the rough-hewn folk from Chase. It was finesse vs. brute force, suspenders vs. shirtsleeves, hand-tooled service vs. ATM's and credit cards.

But the lore lovers missed the real drama. The tension between Chase and Morgan wasn't about cultures; it was about risk. The merger brought together two diametrically opposed views of risk management, one swashbuckling (Chase), the other disciplined and scientific (Morgan). Clearly they could not coexist, and in the immediate aftermath of the merger a battle erupted internally over which view would prevail.[27]

By a market capitalization measure, the merger has not been a success. Between September 2000 and April 2002, the market capitalization of Chase dropped about 37 percent, and more than $40 billion in market value was erased from the combined value of both companies, while the Dow Jones Bank Index rose 6 percent in the same period.

Generally, there is at a least a small culture change or disruption in business process in any acquisition or divestiture due to changed reporting relationships or possibly changes in executive management. The potential extent of these emotions should be observed and probed during the due diligence process and, when possible, carefully reviewed with the human resources and senior executives at the target company. It is very important that during the due diligence process, the review team is extremely careful about understanding the culture and the impact on the individuals. If major culture changes are expected, discuss the changes—on a limited basis—with senior executives at the acquired company. The team should be careful about discussing culture changes with nonexecutive employees at the target company to avoid disrupting the acquisition process before actual decisions are made.

Emotional issues will surface during discussions about existing policies and procedures as well as during discussions about expected changes. It is likely that target company employees will also probe the buying company team as much as possible to gain insight into the culture of the acquiring company. They may discuss human resources policies, employee treatment, corporate fringe benefits, training, and the like. Some of the questions should not be discussed—and these areas should be highlighted to all members of the team.

As an example, if a branded pharmaceutical company were to purchase a generic pharmaceutical company that is a low-cost producer, it is questionable that all the benefits of a high-margin company will be available to the generic target. Team members should be prepared to discuss the theme of the acquisition, that is, product line expansion, geographic expansion, and R&D process acquisition, but not details of the buyer's policies and procedures.

Assume that all published material about the acquiring company would be available to the employees of the target company. The team leader should anticipate the difficult questions and consider preparing acceptable responses before the team due diligence review. This may not be appropriate for all acquisitions, such as territory expansion—in a new country. The buyer would probably not force foreign cultures on the target company.

As with other segments of the integration process, it is important that the members of the due diligence review team understand the concerns of employees at the target company. As team members hear unfavorable comments, they should inform the team leader to ensure that there are no surprises during the negotiation. The due diligence/integration team is an investigative group that also plays the role of ambassador.

Culture Change

Acquisitions may provide an opportunity for introducing a new culture to the acquired company, the acquiring company, or both. As part of the acquisition strategy, executives may assess the culture in both organizations to consider the impact of change. Culture mapping—a simple way to graphically depict the cultures—provides for input from all levels of the organization and focuses on two or three primary characteristics. You will note that this is not an exact science, but rather a pictorial approach to the assessment. The general direction of culture is the goal rather than a specific quantitative analysis. Two axes can be used for plotting: control and creativity. Plotting can be done by location, department, and staff level.

Exhibit 5.1 will visually depict the plot for a company or department. Note that the company culture may vary by location or function. The leadership at the location will have a strong impact on the local culture. As can be seen in the example, culture may also be interpreted differently by employee classification. Major variances in the plot among departments and employees may depict culture problems that must be resolved. The culture map is a picture of the team's assessment of the prevailing culture. A simple graphic can be used to quantify the impression of people—just remember this isn't an exact science but rather a way to capture impressions.

In the book entitled *Managing Mergers, Acquisitions, and Strategic Alliances,* Cartwright and Cooper identified several different types of cultures.[28] As the target company is reviewed, reviewers should categorize the culture as one of these four:

1. Power cultures: Heavily controlled by "the boss" with little self-determination or creativity. Personnel attend the company functions because they must, not because they feel an emotional attachment to the organization. *Easiest to change or merge with.*

2. Role cultures: Impose less control over the individuals than in power cultures. People can relate better to the organization since they influence the ultimate management of the operation. *Easy role-to-role merger. Simple with "light control" culture. Difficult if acquired by strong "power culture."*

3. Task achievement cultures: Employees focus on narrow "deliverables" and obtain satisfaction from completing an individual task. These are control oriented but narrowly focused and are relatively easy to merge.

4. Person/support cultures: Offer the most freedom for self-actualization to the employees. *Most difficult culture to change.*

An example assessment of culture is depicted in Exhibit 5.2. Note that the questions will provide a directional assessment for understanding the culture. In order to be truly effective, a thorough study may be required to assess the company cultures involved in a merger. In the Hewlett-Packard and Compaq merger, "HP began working on cultural issues for a year by creating a so-called strategic change office and by hiring consultants Mercer Delta LLC to do some 'cultural due diligence.' (One finding: HP was more of a voicemail culture, while Compaq was an e-mail culture.)"[29]

However, if the acquirer completes a personal assessment and the due diligence team uses its time wisely, a good gauge of the type of company acquired should result. Informal culture mapping by the due diligence team will provide a general guideline for many organizations. As the reviewers meet with and observe the target company, the team can informally "plot"

EXHIBIT 5.1 Company Culture Maps

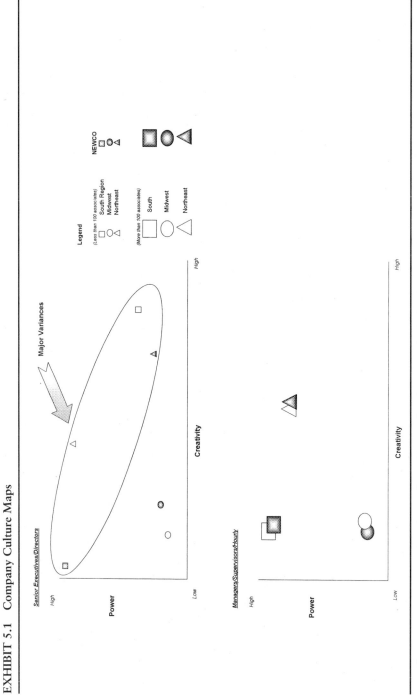

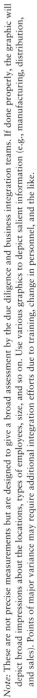

Note: These are not precise measurements but are designed to give a broad assessment by the due diligence and business integration teams. If done properly, the graphic will depict broad impressions about the locations, types of employees, size, and so on. Use various graphics to depict salient information (e.g., manufacturing, distribution, and sales). Points of major variance may require additional integration efforts due to training, change in personnel, and the like.

EXHIBIT 5.2 Cultural Review

Profile: ✓

- Exec:
- Senior Managment
- Middle Management
- Personal Contributor

Location: **Describe:**

Management Orientation

		Rank 1	2	3	4	5	
1	Rigid						Flexible
2	Directive						Participative
3	Bureaucratic						Entrepreneurial
4	Vacillating						Decisive
5	Cautious						Risk-taking
6	Reactive						Proactive
7	Suspicious						Trusting
8	Isolated						Involved
9	Closed-mouth						Open-minded
10	Task-oriented						People-oriented
11	Fragmented						Cohesive
12	Chaotic						Settled
13	Uncaring						Caring
14	Conflictual						Cooperative
15	Uninformative						Informative

		Lo 1	2	3	4	Hi 5
16	Accessibility of Senior Management					
17	Relative autocratic power					
18	Clarity of role definition					
19	Team spirit					
20	Value placed on organization members as individuals					
21	Rules are formalized					
22	Free & unconditional exchange of info					
23	Reliance on authority rather than task experience					
24	Rewards based on task contribution					
25	Formally structured communication channels					
26	Direction or interference from "head office"					

Function: ✓

Primary Activities
- Inbound Logistics
- Operations
- Outbound Logistics
- Marketing

Firm Infrastructure
- General Management
- Planning
- Finance
- MIS

Support Activities
- Procurement
- Technology Development
- Human Resources

27 In this organization, individuals are expected to give 1st priority to:
a. Meeting the challenges of the individual task in which they are involved.
b. Cooperating with and attending to the needs of their fellow workers
c. Following the instuuctions of their superiors.
d. Acting within the parameters of their job description.

28 The organization responds to its members as if they are:
a. Associates or colleagues
b. Family or friends
c. Hired help
d. Contracted employees

29 In this organization, people are motivated and influenced most by:
a. Their own commitment to the task
b. The respect and commitment which they have for their coworkers
c. The prospect of rewards or fear of punishment
d. The company "bible" or rule book

30 A "good" employee is considered to be one who:
a. Is self-motivated and willing to take risks and be innovative if the task demands it.
b. Gets along well with others and is interested in their self-development
c. Always does what his/her boss tells him/her to do without question.
d. Can be relied upon to stick to the company rules

31 Relationships between work units or inter-departmentally are generally:
a. Cooperative
b. Friendly
c. Competitive
d. Indifferent

32 In this organization decisions tend to be:
a. Made by the people on the spot who are close to the problem and have the appropriate expertise
b. Made after considerable discussion and with the consensus of all those involved regardless of their position in the organizational hierarchy.
c. Referred up the line to the person who has the most formal authority.
d. Made by resorting to established precedents.

33 Is most important for a new member of this organization to learn:
a. To use his/her initiative to get the task completed.
b. How to get on with his/her fellow workers.
c. Who really counts in this organization and who comprises the political coalitions.
d. The formal rules and regulations.

34 The dominant managerial style of this organization is:
a. Democratic and open
b. Supportive and responsive to individual needs and idiosyncrasies
c. Authoritarian
d. Impersonal and remote

the cultural assessment of the individual plants, departments, or country operations on the control/creativity matrix. Smaller circles indicate, for example, a lower number of employees than do larger circles. As these informal "maps" are accumulated, a graphic picture should become evident. If no significant skewing surfaces, the dominant culture should have a major impact on the integration process.

Despite all efforts made to describe and properly interpret the culture of target companies, the efforts sometimes fail. Cisco has often been cited as a master of successful acquisition and integration, but sometimes even the "master" can fail.

It was an all-too-typical deal for Cisco Systems Inc. Monterey Networks Inc., an optical-routing startup in which Cisco held a minority stake, was a quarry with no revenue, no products, and no customers—just millions in losses it had racked up since its founding in 1997. Despite those deficits, Cisco plunked down a half-billion dollars in stock to buy the rest of the company in 1999.

But within days of closing the deal, all three of Monterey's founders, including its engineering guru and chief systems architect, walked out the door, taking with them millions of dollars in gains from the sale. "I came to the realization I wasn't going to have any meaningful impact on the product by staying," said. H. Michael Zadikian, a Monterey founder. Eighteen months later, Cisco shut down the business altogether, sacking the rest of the management team and taking a $108 million write-off.[30]

As these analyses are prepared, don't be overwhelmed by the process. The goal is to think about the "culture question" and observe the company in action. This is a very soft assessment.

These maps can be prepared using several different criteria. For example, the size of the circle can designate the size of the departments, locations (if color-coded), or possibly the levels in the organization chart. As these "snapshots" are captured, patterns may be observed.

Exhibit 5.2 will show how easy or difficult a merger will be based on an assessment of the culture type.

In order to have an orderly transition from one culture to another, the dominant culture must be defined, and a detailed plan for transition should be prepared. The plan should include timelines for assessment, training, and execution of the changes.

Transition Teams: Buyer/Seller

Honesty and integrity must be part of the review process and communication. In order to ensure that the tone and direction of communication are proper *coaching may be required on both sides of the acquisition.* For example, inside or confidential information should be identified for the due diligence team to ensure that it is not disclosed to the target. Guidelines discussing what can or cannot be disclosed should be developed, since the review team most likely includes several functional areas. Exhibit 5.3

EXHIBIT 5.3 Information Summary: Target Company Questions (Examples)

Number	Reference	Description	Response
1.0	General	Do you generally leave the organization alone - without change?	Each organization that is acquired has unique characteristics. Our goal is to improve shareholder value by making good decisions about people and structure based on the facts available. There is no standard, except a thorough review of each situation.
2.0	Human Resources	How do you determine your pay scales?	Pay scales are industry and location specific. Compensation levels are tested annually to ensure equity.
		What are the vacation policies at the acquiring company?	Vacation policies are not discussed with target companies. However, the company goal is to be in the top quartile for the industry/region for compensation and fringe benefits.
		Do you have educational support programs?	Again, our objective is to be in the top quartile for the region and industry for all our benefit programs. We will be reviewing the current programs and adjust accordingly.
3.0	Manufacturing	Do you believe in "lean manufacturing" practices?	

Develop the Q&A in a brainstorming session, or assign responsibility for Q&A to functional execs. Retain all the historical Q&A for future acquisitions, and update for all the new questions that may arise in an acquisition.

includes some hypothetical questions and answers that may be discussed during any on-site discussions between a buyer and a target company.

At all points of contact with the target company, it is important that only motivated, concerned people be allowed to meet with the target company personnel. Imagine how difficult it would be to complete the acquisition if a "bad attitude" represented the company in the review. Confidentiality is also essential in any acquisition contact—it must be emphasized that all information is strictly confidential.

During initial discussions with the target, think about the "to be" organization and the kind of culture required. Ideally, the "to be" organization will be the one with the best operation (e.g., the best MIS operation). It is not always the largest organization that will dominate the acquisition. In fact, it may be strategically important to select the target to lead some functional areas to demonstrate the openness to change. The acquisition team leader should ensure that the review is carefully organized to avoid alienating either organization. Sometimes the surviving organization will vary with function or location, since a particular function within a company may not have a consistent high-quality performance. For example, while the HR function at the buyer may have the best people and processes, the target may have superior people and processes in manufacturing operations.

Transition Leadership

During the initial acquisition phase, reporting relationships and chain of command should be established as soon as is practical. If temporary reporting relationships or a temporary organization chart is established, there should be a sunset term—an end—for the temporary status. For example, a public disclosure to the organization may state that for the next ninety days there will be an acting CEO in the organization or an acting CEO of the combined entity. Guidelines for these temporary responsibilities will be helpful for the temporary leaders. Examples of such guidelines may include capital and expense spending approval levels, hiring/firing controls, compensation and bonus payment approvals required, and organization changes. Think through and manage the timing of the sunset term to improve the chance of a successful integration. Establish mileposts or deliverables for the temporary executives to reinforce their management role. Planning and timely execution will reinforce the credibility of the transition management team.

ORGANIZATION DEVELOPMENT

Review the existing organization charts, *including open and filled positions,* to understand the potential impact of the consolidation on the organization and the personnel. A comparison of the organization charts by function, location, level, and type of responsibility can help to identify organizational priorities. Although it is a detailed technical exercise, it is one component of defining the final company consolidation—the "to be" configuration. As you complete the review, consider the variables that can affect the organization, including future acquisitions and employee turnover. See Exhibits 5.4 and 5.5 for examples of alternate methods to summarize the organizations.

Visualizing the organization in various summary formats will provide a different perspective of the operation. The summaries may also show new information about the target company. Exhibit 5.4 displays the organization from the highest to lowest level. This particular example shows the span of control allowed, the designed supervisor:worker ratio, and the number of layers of management. In Exhibit 5.5, a high ratio of contract employees may reflect high growth, adverse HR conditions, high turnover, or extremely limited resources. In each case, you may want some additional review to be sure that you understand the root cause.

Please remember there is no single best method. *Use judgment,* and be sure that you focus on the primary reason for the acquisition and the specific companies involved. The critical areas that should be considered in almost any review are:

- Number of levels in each organization
- Descriptors of the organization, including full time (equivalents) and contract (temporary workers)
- Filled and open positions
- Summaries by location
- Summaries by function
- Summaries by type of responsibility—senior/middle management or other
- Professional (college or technically trained) or other (clerical, blue collar or non-specialized).

The number of levels within an organization may vary dramatically between the buyer and seller—from very centralized to decentralized. Organizations may also vary by type—functional, product line, or perhaps regional. Each organization should be defined and analyzed, and a final "to be" organization should be determined based on the goals of the combined organization. Once defined, the optimum organization should be plotted, including number of levels, number of people, structure (e.g., the number of managers), functions (internal and external), and geographic structure. The organization charts should reflect regions or territories as well as product lines, divisions, and functions. All major organizational components of the target and the acquirer should be considered in the review.

EXHIBIT 5.4 Organization Master Plan

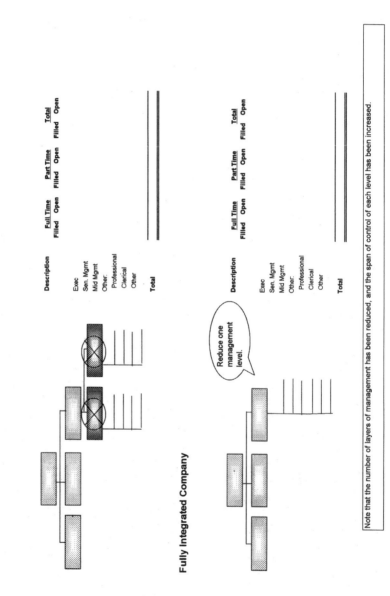

Current Target Company

Description	Full Time		Part Time		Total	
	Filled	Open	Filled	Open	Filled	Open
Exec						
Sen. Mgmt						
Mid Mgmt						
Other:						
Professional						
Clerical						
Other						
Total						

Reduce one management level.

Fully Integrated Company

Description	Full Time		Part Time		Total	
	Filled	Open	Filled	Open	Filled	Open
Exec						
Sen. Mgmt						
Mid Mgmt						
Other:						
Professional						
Clerical						
Other						
Total						

Note that the number of layers of management has been reduced, and the span of control of each level has been increased.

94

EXHIBIT 5.5 Organization Description

Regional/Location
Northeast

| | Type of Employee | | | | | | |
| Description | Full Time | | Part Time | | Contract | | Total | |
	Filled	Open	Filled	Open	Filled	Open	Filled	Open
Exec								
Sen. Mgmt								
Mid Mgmt								
Other:								
Professional								
Clerical								
Other								
Total								

Consider the number of Part-Time and Contract positions. They may provide insight into the Target Company personnel policies.

These may also be the easiest to combine with an existing organization. Also, since Part-Time and Contract positions may not be a part of the normal payroll, the responsibilities and tasks completed may be missed if not specifically requested.

Functional
Sales

| | Type of Employee | | | | | | |
| Description | Full Time | | Part Time | | Contract | | Total | |
	Filled	Open	Filled	Open	Filled	Open	Filled	Open
Exec								
Sen. Mgmt								
Mid Mgmt								
Other:								
Professional								
Clerical								
Other								
Total								

Review the organization in many different views - for example by location, by function, and by type of personnel. Pay attention to the number of open, filled, and contract positions.

Although creating an organization that accomplishes the strategic goal is the final result, there may be temporary or short-term changes that must be implemented to reach the strategic goal. Temporary changes considered should also be reviewed by the due diligence review team and approved by the team leader. Temporary change plans should be reviewed with responsible management of the target company, when appropriate. For example, if the MIS director position is open at the target company, a temporary MIS director from the acquiring company may be assigned to maintain the operation until a permanent substitute can be placed. As these changes are identified, implementation teams should be established and carefully managed to ensure that there is no significant disruption in either side of the transaction.

Organization: Strategic Review

In the long-term or strategic time frame, it is important to understand why the company has been acquired. It is important that the organization review and the evaluation of individual employees are unbiased. The lack of bias is essential to maintain credibility. It may be appropriate to hire outside consultants to provide this unbiased review of selected key employees. Selection of outside consultants will be determined by the tone of the acquisition, the depth of the management assessing the target, and the potential overlap of future responsibilities.

During the planning of the HP and Compaq merger, the leaders apparently assessed the structure, organization, and "to be" aspects of the merged company.

Two of every three middle-management appointments recently made by Hewlett-Packard Co went to its executives over managers from the acquired Compaq Computer Corp., according to an analysis of the latest appointments.

In a few of the new groups, the appointments are split fairly evenly between the two—such as Network Storage and its industry and corporate account portion of its big-computer unit. Elsewhere, the appointments are a patchwork of HP and Compaq teams that mirror the individual companies' market-share rankings.

"Where Compaq is strong, they kept the team, and kept the products. Where Compaq is weak, they went to HP," said Terry Shannon, who writes a computer industry newsletter called Shannon Knows HPC.[31]

During a review of the organization, it may be worthwhile to establish an immediate hiring freeze in both organizations. A hiring freeze will create time for effective analysis and decision making, provide some flexibility for internal transfer, and reinforce your concern for the employees. The freeze should be brief—that is, no more than thirty days. If extended beyond thirty days, there will be uncertainty in both organizations, which may result in poor morale, poor performance, and unwanted employee turnover. As two organizations are combined, people in other functional areas may satisfy job requirements in the recruiting organization.

For example, a small target company may have a marketing department with an exceptional graphic designer who has successfully created packaging and labels for their products. That individual may be able to satisfy a marketing department need in the acquirer for an advertising graphic artist. In this case, a headcount freeze and a review of the talent pools may avoid a termination with associated costs, and a hiring with associated costs. Administration personnel, human resources, and finance personnel often can work in many departments.

An effective organization review will be quick and concise and will consider the resources available and the "to be" organization requirements. The review should consider the entire organization: board members, executives, and all other employees, U.S. and foreign. The review should also consider contract agents that may not even appear on an organization chart but are critical elements of the business process. Listing all of the functions and levels in each organization is a way to complete the organizational review. The analysis should be used to summarize the total company after completion of the transition plan. The process is an iterative process, which may require several working versions to capture the true integrated structure. Each employee transition will send a message to the organization.

Note in Exhibit 5.6 that all levels of the organization have been identified and separated by functional area, identified by individual company, and the combined company. In the example, the integrated portion of the graphic summarizes to less than a combined total—which reflects expected synergy, for example, in finance and legal. The combined portion of the spreadsheet will result from an understanding of the strategic intent of the acquisition and an analysis of functions and locations. For example, if the strategic intent of the acquisition is to acquire the R&D personnel in the organization, R&D will not be decreased. Other areas may also be affected.

In the example, it is also obvious that board members and senior executives in some functional areas may not be required. A summary may also be prepared to reflect regional concentrations and to better understand the impact of combining the geographic operations. Although synergy may result from organizations being combined in a given country or region, it is not necessarily true that they will be eliminated in total.

Contract Agents and Open Positions

One factor often overlooked in the integration process is contract agents. Contract agents—temps—can have either formal, legal commitments or informal, temporary ones. Some employees in today's market are

EXHIBIT 5.6   Organizational Review: Integration Planning (Headcount Summary)

Description	Company A	Company B	Combined	Fully Integrated	Comments
Board Members	7	9	16	8	
CEO	1	1	2	1	
Research & Development	40	15	55	45	Reduction due to duplication in Microbiology lab. R&D reduction of 10.
Product Development Process Technology Personnel Intellectual Property					
Human Resources Development	15	4	19	18	Reduce VP HR at acquired company. Policy level will be handled by parent.
Administration Compensation Strategy Personnel Development					
Inbound Logistics	15	5	20	20	Constant force required due to separate plant location.
Purchasing Inventory Handling Inbound Shipping					
Operations	400	180	580	550	Will eliminate duplicate QA testing lab.
Production Outsourced					
Outbound Logistics	25	5	30	25	Outbound logistics will be concentrated in parent company.
Warehousing Shipping					
Sales & Marketing	50	5	55	55	
Dealer Support & Customer Service	10	15	25	30	Target has very successful International Dealer network which will be expanded.
Infrastructure Activities	25	10	35	30	
Accounting					
Total	580	239	819	773	

Once you've defined what is important to you, compile the statistics for a broad image of what may be done. Concentrate on industry metrics, such as Sales/headcount, Profit/headcount, and Service reps/customer base. Note that the summary of functions is identical to Exhibit 3.3.

temporary because they have taken early retirement, but they may provide essential services using critical skills unavailable elsewhere in the company. Think about these temps and the services they provide—can you afford to miss this classification of employee?

The organization review must also consider all open positions. Open positions should be frozen until you understand what the "to be" organization will look like. Each open position should be evaluated based on the job description, functional responsibilities, and company needs. Open positions should be reviewed as soon as possible to decide if people should be hired. It is important to be decisive in the analysis to reinforce the importance of the individual and the need to move the process along.

Define the Optimum Organization Chart

The optimum organization chart may require several iterations. For example, the strategic intent of the organization may be to strengthen the R&D function. However, to achieve that goal, several iterations of combining businesses must be completed. You may want to consider a time-phased analysis. A time-phased analysis—that is, a bi-annual summary of the organizations—will provide the perspective necessary to complete major reorganizations. As you establish organizational targets for several years, you can plot the organization at periodic intervals.

As the organization charts are reviewed, factors such as employee training, tenure, and performance ratings within the organization should be a part of the decision process. If historical performance ratings are not available, consider developing them immediately to ensure that reasonable, consistent evaluations are available for personnel decisions. The responsible functional management should review each iteration of review as well as the overall goal of the combined business to ensure a consistent understanding of the process. While this may sound like a cumbersome process, it is important to maintain management control over the combining of the organizations. Remember that both organizations are subject to declining morale.

The optimum organization chart will result from a review of available resources and from comparison to the strategic intent of the combined operation. An essential part of this analysis will be input from the due diligence review team, since they are the first set of observers at the target company. Each individual on the due diligence review team will be required to identify essential players within the functional areas. The functional executives are the most knowledgeable about the future organization and the strategic goal of the acquisition. These selections can be done based on the review of organizational needs, the strategic intent of the acquisition, discussion with essential executives and the target company, and so on.

International Operations

International operations represent unique challenges for most U.S. businesses. Many countries are much more socially oriented than the United States. For example, in the Scandinavian countries, Germany, Spain, Italy, and France, it is nearly impossible to terminate employees without unusually large severance benefits. Existing laws or prevailing industry business practice may require a company to pay a multiple of annual profit to a distributor to sever a business relationship. Country law or customary practice is designed to protect local businesses in developing countries from unfair practices of major companies. Make sure that country experts review the organization changes to be sure of the cost and impact on the remaining company.

In some countries, distributors and contract agents have onerous termination costs. How many times have companies been subjected to significant termination settlements unknowingly?

QUICK CHECK OF CHAPTER 5

✓ Employees

✓ Buyer

✓ Target

✓ Employee leaders

✓ Culture assessment

✓ Define "to be" organization

6

People, Compensation, and Benefits: Understand the Issues

People drive company results. Acquisitions potentially present significant issues related to employee business processes. Depending on the type of acquisition, there may be concern about effective payroll processing, commission plans, bonuses, and long-term compensation programs. Personal concerns in many acquisitions can involve both the acquiring and target companies' employees. Personal concerns can include worries about job security, personal expectations for career growth within the company, merit raises, or perhaps even long-standing reporting relationships, which may be eliminated.

Employee benefits and personal compensation components are important to both the acquiring and acquired companies' employees. As an acquisition progresses, it is important to establish a strategy for employee benefits and compensation and to communicate the strategy to the employees. The team approach, which includes participants from both sides of the acquisition and a selection of functional areas, will provide responsible input to establish ongoing tactical plans and strategies to meet employee needs.

Compensation and benefits are the most personal activities to the individual employees and therefore are the most significant area to be reviewed early in the integration process. A thorough analysis of actual and perceived benefits at both companies will ensure that there are no major missteps in the final integration.

Compensation and benefits planning is very important because it has a direct, immediate, and personal impact on each employee. Compensation planning should include monetary as well as nonmonetary rewards and perquisites. Each company organizational level, location, and classification of employee should be considered for review on a prioritized basis. The human resources representatives, who are responsible for coordinating compensation and benefits, should develop short-range and long-range plans. These plans should be reviewed for all locations, comparing both acquiring and acquired companies.

Support systems such as time reporting, project accounting, and other employee time-driven management reporting may require substantial systems support. Initially, such critical processes can be identified during the due diligence review. In any review, support systems that are essential for the effective management of the business should be identified and analyzed, and the task force should immediately prepare action plans for successful integration.

The first steps of this kind of review can be completed during the due diligence planning process, followed by a more detailed formal review immediately after completing the acquisition. Be sure that all communications channels—both to and from employees—are open, and be sure that the task force is responsive to questions at all times. One solution to open communication would be to establish an intranet/Internet to have responses to questions and comments/concerns from all levels of employees documented in a timely, consistent, and professional way. HR questions should be coordinated through the human resources representatives on the task force. Once the communications process is implemented, the process should be properly maintained—that is, updated frequently. Approved responses to inquiries and technical questions should be prepared and communicated on a timely basis. A word of caution: Open communications may accelerate the transition process by raising issues that the companies have not anticipated or that address sensitive areas that the company is not prepared to discuss. If you have a hostile takeover or expect many challenging issues to be raised, carefully consider the extent of opening the communications channel.

As the employee communications channel is opened, manage the channel as if it contains a market research opportunity for the transition process. Think about the kind of information that may be available: the number and type of questions and the source of questions (location, employee level, functional area). As the channel is opened, information can be analyzed to understand the broad sentiment of the employees. As certain types of questions intensify, it may be worthwhile to prepare a single press release that provides strategic direction, perhaps some concrete statements about the issues, and approximate timing of activity. It is not essential that every individual question be answered but rather that the information discussing the company's intent be available to the employees.

PAYROLL AND DIRECT COMPENSATION

Payroll and other compensation are among the most critical elements to be considered once the acquisition is completed. Compensation is important to all employees because they need the cash and it is a scorecard reflecting their importance to the company. Acquisitions can take many forms, including the purchase of entire companies or segments of a company. Buying an entire company requires less payroll planning, since the existing systems may be used until a formal review to determine the best action can be completed and transition plans can be prepared if required.

Alternatively, buying a division or business segment from a company becomes much more complex. New systems may be required to compensate employees, since the existing systems may not be available for continued use. Most times, however, temporary arrangements may be made with the "seller" to continue payroll processing for a fee.

Employees must be paid on a timely and continuous basis throughout any transition. The "backroom process" transition for payroll and benefits should be as invisible as possible to the employees during any transition period. Many processes will likely change in the integration—but make the compensation and benefits transition as simple as possible. Don't disrupt or change the processing unless it's essential. If you do change, be sure to thoroughly explain the changes to the employees. Any disruption in the compensation and fringe benefits will receive an immediate bad reaction from the employees. Can the transition process afford to have a strike, a business slowdown, or dramatic changes in efficiency?

If you identify major compensation and fringe differences between the target company and the acquirer, it may be appropriate to buy out existing plans at the target company. This may appear to be expensive initially, but treating the employees fairly and maintaining a single compensation process and structure may justify the cost. Tabulate the excess costs since one-time accounting treatment may be possible.

Payroll

Payroll transitions can be processed by services such as Paychex, ADP, or other automated processing services. These organizations provide full-service payroll systems, online reporting, training, and more to simplify the changes. Transitions may include changes in FICA withholding, federal ID numbers, and accumulated or current 401k or pension contributions. Changes that affect the employees—such as a change of company employer in midyear—may have a personal cost to the employees for government-mandated programs such as FICA, federal unemployment, and state unemployment. The smart companies will reimburse these costs so the changes have a zero cost to the employees. Review all the programs to identify the issues, and prepare a game plan to resolve any unusual features. Once any changes are identified, discuss the changes with the employees.

A company's payroll can be weekly, semimonthly, biweekly, and monthly. Each type of payroll should be considered separately, since the employees may be affected by the timing. The buyer company's human resources representatives should review the process with focus groups from each payroll grade/classification. Ideally the groups would include some opinion leaders. It is important that the plans involve the target company employees so that they are assisting in the process change. This allows for sharing in the benefits (blame) during the transition. If employees are included from the target company and the company is responsive to issues raised, it will be evident that the acquiring company intends to do a fair job.

As payrolls are changed, paychecks, withholding statements, and some forms may be different. A reference list of *don'ts*:

- Don't forget to train the employees.
- Don't forget to have qualified personnel available to answer questions.
- Don't be afraid to have a hotline.

It is important that all employees receive proper training and guidance related to the changes. Problem prevention will be much less expensive and emotional, so plan ahead.

A master list of all payrolls and benefits should be prepared and stratified or sorted in a meaningful way—such as by type of employee. An example is shown in Exhibit 6.1. The list should be based on the acquired company's organization charts.

Payroll documents and procedures should be obtained, reviewed, and summarized to reflect the 5 W's: Who? What? When? Where? and Why? The packages of information should include forms, timing, approvals, and "where used" information. Invite personnel at the target company to prepare the summary of their operations—what better source than the current employees? Of course, the acquiring company personnel will be familiar with their own procedures, and working with the acquirer's employees can only improve the integration plans for the company. See Exhibit 6.2 for further information.

This spreadsheet can be expanded to include locations, payroll processor, timing, and the like. Preparation of summaries allows for stratification by groups based on common information. A "master schedule" that reflects every compensation transaction is the best method to avoid a missed employee or agent.

As the spreadsheet is prepared, you may find unusual compensation programs not previously identified. As an example, gain-sharing in a Michigan manufacturing plant may be a pilot program being tested at the target company. This would be identified in a summary of every compensation transaction.

EXHIBIT 6.1   Compensation Summary: Target Company

| | # Employees | Location | Compensation Programs | | | | |
			Payroll	Commission	Bonus	Long Term Compensation	Options
Board of Directors							
Chair	1	Various	A				
Audit Committee	3	Various	B				
Compensation Committee	3	Various	C				
All Other			D				
Executives							
President	1		E		F	G	H
VP - General Counsel	1		I		J	G	H
VP - Sales	1		I		J	G	H
VP - All Other	6		I		J	G	H
Middle Management							
Directors	45		I		J		K
Managers - 1	50		I				
Managers - 2	75		I				
Managers - 3	10		I				
All Others							
Other Employees	750		I				
Contract Agents	5						
Total	**951**						

Reference to more detailed plans attached.

A master summary should be prepared to ensure that all classifications of employees at the target company have been properly considered. This should include temps, consultants, and contract employees. Remember to include all locations.

EXHIBIT 6.2 Payroll Summary: Checklist for Compensation Transition

Payroll Description	Frequency	Systems Linkage	Date Due	Done By	Forms Description	Reference	Approvals	Service	Bank Account
Chicago Hourly	Weekly	Standard cost system	Mon: 9:00 AM	ADP	Timesheet		1.1 Supervisor	DD/Check	Nations Bank
Executive	Monthly		1st Tues - 9:00 AM	ADP				DD/Check	1st National
Incentive	Quarterly	Sales Reports	2nd Tues	Fin	Summary		1.3 COO	Check	1st National
Bonus	Annual	P&L + Performance Summary	3rd Friday - Year End	Fin	P&L		1.4 CEO	Check	1st National

Define what is important information, and capture all the date..... Focus is on Who? What? When? Where? How? ....

Note: The above represents the details of all accounts used to compensate employees at the Chicago operation. It is important to identify the critical elements of the compensation systems due to timing, linkage, and possible changes that may be required. The linkage area indicates that other systems may be affected by a change in basic payroll systems. Also, the approvals need a change due to the change in organization structure.

Assume that all employees will expect the highest level of compensation, regardless of the resulting company shape, size, or ultimate configuration, after the integration is complete. If two companies are combined in the same city, employees will expect that the highest compensation structures and levels will certainly be used. Employees will discuss compensation levels among themselves and compare levels to the other company's.

Commission Plans

Commission plans, if properly designed, provide incentives for the sales force to deliver excellent performance and drive the company to superior profitability. During any transition period, commission plans should initially be left intact as much as possible, since reps have committed to the goals and measurements already established. Most likely, they have prepared a sales plan and an established pipeline to optimize their compensation based on the formulas. If in the short term you need to make changes to the commission, err on the generous side, and don't disrupt the sales pipeline and the informal communications channel to your customers. Since the sales reps are the front line to the world—customers, clients, and competitors—it is important that the sales organizations have minimal disruption. *Sales reps are driven by self-starting motivation. Keep them upbeat, motivated, and focused on the right targets.*

As with all compensation and benefits, the commission plans should be compared between the combining organizations. If one plan is better than the other, you should anticipate questions from the apparently lesser-paid individuals whether or not they are actually paid less. Be assured that both sales organizations will exchange the details of their respective plans. Broad dispersion among the features of the plans will cause problems, so plan to resolve the issues and communicate to the employees. If one organization uses an irresponsibly generous program (i.e., the target, since the acquirer, who is also the reviewer, is unlikely to consider its program irresponsible), the integration team must address the excessive compensation immediately. Delays in the compensation area will cause lingering motivational problems.

Considering the variety of commission plans available—with specific performance goals, which may be sales or order values, or nonmonetary goals regarding sales calls or new accounts—the transition plan should be carefully constructed to avoid any disruption in overall sales performance. Carefully coordinate the integration among the senior management of all the involved companies, since both organizations must be satisfied that challenging yet fair goals are established for the sales organizations.

If significant changes are required because of a dramatic change in the basic business, consider a buyout of the existing plan, based on seasonal adjustments, new product introductions, and the like. The buyout should be fair and should be perceived as fair by affected employees. For example, if a smaller company is acquired by a larger, more sophisticated company, the acquirer may have a dramatically different commission plan, with multiple control points—for example, the sales pipeline of new accounts, year-over-year account growth, and new product introductions. The smaller company may be driven by shorter-term goals that emphasize monthly sales and cash flow targets, and consequently efforts on strategic selling may be minimal. Larger companies may dedicate more time to strategic selling, which can include trade shows, public relations efforts, and cold calls on new customers or industries.

Once the major differences are identified, the senior HR and sales management representatives should determine:

- Baseline compensation and expectations of the reps
- Future strategies of the company (e.g., blends of short-term tactical activity and long-range goals such as participation in trade shows)
- A buyout plan that is equitable (and possibly generous) to maintain the positive momentum of the transition
- Training requirements to provide the tools necessary to achieve the goals (goals must not be modified until the proper groundwork has been established)
- Full-scale training, which should be implemented for all affected reps

A compensation expert (whether an in-house or outside consultant) should review the plan.

The commission plans should consider products, selling prices, and gross margins, as well as regional coverage. In addition, *the commission plans should reflect a "fair" set of goals, as well as compensation.* Regional and industry norms can be used as a basis for benchmarking, when the final commission plans are prepared.

Bonus Plans

Bonus plans are very sensitive business drivers, since the plans often are targeted to senior management performance for the year and for measurable components of long-term strategy. Bonus plans can be very broad and include current compensation, deferred compensation, stock benefits, and other forms of compensation. Bonus plans should be reviewed carefully by senior management and board members at each company to be sure that the senior management is properly aligned. Transition bonus plans should be constructed to ensure that they are fair and equitable to both organizations. It is not just the acquired company that will suffer from morale problems, if plans are inequitable.

All bonus plans should be reviewed to determine if they are designed to motivate through current or future benefits. Bonus programs' current benefits should be reviewed first to be sure that current activities deliver the expected results. Future or long-term benefits drive performance to strategic goals. Although secondary, these goals should be adjusted to reflect combined businesses for executives who will bear similar responsibilities in the future. The initial impact of a combination of businesses may result with an adjustment to the current year performance and with changes to strategic deliverables. The tone of review and discussion should be such that participants in both companies will realize that *a fair review is underway.*

The bonus plans will often affect the most senior management in the organization and may include members of the boards of directors, who are company investors. Key executive bonus plans should be reviewed and modified to update the strategic goals for the combined businesses. Since these plan reviews affect the highest management levels, it may be appropriate to use independent, outside consultants to obtain an unbiased review and to ensure equitable treatment. A modest investment in an unbiased review may prove to be a great investment to accelerate the transition process and to provide immediate motivation for the key executives.

Other Compensation

During the past decade, companies have become more creative in compensating key personnel. Programs now include features such as deferred compensation plans, extended pension benefits, stock grants and options programs, and personal use of aircraft, vacation homes, and so on. Each of these unique features will complicate a comparison among companies. Again, the overriding concern should be "fairness" in any compensation program. Employees who receive these unusual forms of compensation awards are usually the leaders, who will ensure the success of the future operation. As a result, the review and analysis may require high-level negotiations and concessions. Independent consultants should be used to avoid bias and confirm a high-quality review. This will allow the key managers to focus on business operations rather than their personal wealth.

All forms of compensation should be summarized on a checklist for compensation transition (see Exhibit 6.2). Any factors necessary for the proper and timely preparation and delivery of the compensation should be listed on the schedule. Again, if all forms of compensation are listed, all critical elements will be reviewed for proper transition.

PERSONNEL PERFORMANCE REVIEWS

Well-managed companies nurture their employees' career development through well-developed performance review processes. Documented performance reviews will be a solid foundation for understanding goals and objectives, and also a means to identify the quality of target company personnel. The status of all personnel performance reviews should be documented as soon as possible—perhaps initially during the due diligence review process for key employees. If no reviews are prepared, the target company is not effectively managing one of its most important assets—its employees. If reviews are prepared and are of low quality, the company management processes will require focus and attention. If the reviews are of high quality, consider yourself lucky—a major culture change may not be required. If no appraisals have been completed, draft appraisals focused on key criteria should be prepared to ensure that employees are a part of the transition process. During periods of transition, individual employees will seek the tradition as a stabilizing force. Employees who have not yet received performance reviews for a recent period before the transition may consider their past efforts lost if they are not reviewed by the current company management. The HR transition team should identify the current status of reviews and, whenever possible, obtain up-to-date performance summaries. A documented assessment—or a cutoff summary of performance for an interim period—will ensure that there is a reasonable transition for the individual employee.

Personnel performance reviews should be considered as a basis for promotion. If an acquired company does not have an existing documented performance system, informal reviews should be completed for key personnel as soon as possible. Informal reviews will often be the norm in small, less rigidly managed companies. If a company does not use a formal evaluation process, the philosophy and value of appraisals may not be properly understood.

Be sure to obtain current documented reviews of all supervisory and higher personnel, since these people will be leading the transition efforts. The reviews should preferably be recent and should reflect performance versus established goals. If the target company either does not have a process to review or does not have current reviews, the HR teams should require that brief reviews be prepared in a standard format. There are several benefits to the review process:

1. Employees will recognize the importance of the reviews and the desire to have a current summary of their performance.

2. Management at the target company can demonstrate the management skill at performance assessment and can provide current insight into the skills of key employees. This will acquaint the acquiring company with the management skills in the acquired company.

3. The review can be used as a basis for early identification of key personnel and as the basis of succession planning for the combined business.

The personnel performance reviews in many large companies are often structured, often specifically measure performance against established goals, and assess personal attributes such as communication and leadership skills.

Personnel performance reviews should be modified to the best process from either company as early as possible. For example, if an acquired company is not accustomed to a structured performance review and the acquiring company has a formal review process, the target company process should be upgraded to the "higher level" as soon as practicable. A near-term implementation is better than a long delay since the process will improve the management process.

If the acquired company does not have a formal review system, training will be required. Training for preparation of personnel reviews is much more extensive than just filling in a form and requires a thorough understanding of company goals, goal-setting priorities, and important management attributes such as organization skills, leadership, communication, and technical skills. Proper training should concentrate on the motivational basis of the personnel review system as well as on guidance in review techniques by supervisors and managers. Whatever you do, don't ask employees to perform the review function without proper training. If you do, the process will be demotivating, ineffective, and inefficient to the surviving organization.

Quick performance review transitions will require training and perhaps establishing performance goals for the near term or remainder of the year. The human resources personnel should coordinate the evaluation process and training. The performance review process should:

1. Establish a goal-setting methodology, based on the established near-term and strategic goals.
2. Define a suitable performance review process (forms, timing, definitions, and thorough understanding).
3. Implement the training for the new process.
4. Establish meaningful goals that will meet business objectives.
5. Implement the review process.

Procedures should first focus on the goal-setting and review process, then the formal goal-setting activity, such as specific deliverables for the corporation, individual departments, and people. These forms should be modified so that the acquired company can more easily adapt them to its culture. Remember, the "best system"—whether that of the acquiring company or the acquired company—should be adopted as soon as possible.

For those not familiar with a documented evaluation process, Exhibit 6.3 reflects several areas that may be useful to review. Note that there are only ten items rated, providing focus for the individual. Also, there are "tangible" and "other items" measured. These can vary by company and type of responsibility. Measurable items are less subject to interpretation and may be easiest to buy out in any transition plan. Remember that a company may have a different focus for performance based on its strategy—for example, a growing company may focus on new accounts, while an established

EXHIBIT 6.3 Performance Reviews: Examples

	Rating (Hi = 5)	Weighting (Base 100%)	Value
Deliverables			
Achieve sales of $3 million per quarter	4	20%	0.8
Achieve Gross Margin of at least 50%	4	10%	0.4
Achieve Contribution Margin (after direct expenses) of at least $1 million per quarter	3	5%	0.2
Other Activities			
Open at least 3 accounts with minimum sales of $50 thousand per quarter	2	10%	0.2
Attend at least one trade show per quarter	5	10%	0.5
Attend at least one training session re: sales operations per quarter	3	5%	0.2
Subtotal		**60%**	**2.3**
Personal Attributes			
Verbal communications	3	5%	0.2
Written communications	4	10%	0.4
Delegation & management processes	3	15%	0.5
Organization skills	5	10%	0.5
Subtotal		**40%**	**1.6**
Total		**100%**	**3.9**

Rating is an assessment of performance based on a 1-5 scale, with "5" being best. The weighting represents the importance to the particular function - note that Sales & Margin represent more than one-third of the total deliverables, while new accounts and developing business represent another 25%. Personal attributes represent the skills required for the individual to grow in his or her career.

company may concentrate on account retention or sales/product increases. The "weighting factor," which represents relative importance of the particular attribute or goal, as a percent of total performance, allows management to concentrate the greatest effort on those areas considered most important.

Factors that should be considered in any performance review plan include:

- Limit the number of items to a manageable number. Too many measurement factors are distracting. Just as a business must prioritize, individual goals should be blended to achieve company objectives.

- Quantitative as well as qualitative factors should be considered goals. Although it is often difficult to rate qualitative activities, it is worthwhile to add them to modify personal performance and improve career development.

- Personal characteristics are important features of any performance measurement system. If the performance review is designed to coordinate business performance goals and to encourage personal development, development characteristics significant to the job should be reviewed.

Weighting by percent at the personal level will focus on the most significant performance criteria. A high percent indicates that these are the most important to the company. Again, this prioritizes the most important activities for the individual.

Characteristics are more judgmental and subject to interpretation by the supervisor. These generally are designed to enhance the employee's productivity in a position. During any transition plan, each of these areas should be reviewed on a current basis—for example, within 3–6 months of the transition. This will ensure that an employee has feedback about his or her performance before major changes in operating control have been fully implemented and absorbed.

Each personnel review will allow the new company to determine the best method to introduce new goals for the combined operation. Once the performance review process is understood, critical goals for the combined company can be prepared. The initial goals of the company should include objectives for the integration process. While it would be nice to have fully documented, recent appraisals, it sometimes is just not practical. If they aren't available, develop a broad assessment concentrating on the most important features for the "to be" company and make a quick assessment.

EMPLOYEE BENEFITS

As the benefits are summarized, management should consider the potential savings available that may result from the combination. The company cost may be reduced due to increased buying leverage, which could allow either for additional benefits at no additional cost or for overall cost reductions for the benefits programs.

A complete summary of all benefits at both the acquiring and the acquired company is very important at the outset. The tabulation should be segregated by type of benefit—for example, life insurance, health insurance, 401k, pension plan, and tuition assistance—to insure that broad categories have been properly considered for both organizations. No one within the organization will be receptive to reduced benefits because of a transition or acquisition. As these benefits are summarized and documented, consider stratifying the benefits to reflect employee organization levels such as hourly, supervisory, managerial, and directorial. Benefits will likely vary among the organization levels, and you will want to understand the various offerings before any changes are made. The summary should include all significant business segments such as locations, employee classifications, and product lines.

The benefits should be analyzed in relation to regional and industry requirements to insure those reasonable benefits are in place after the transition. Although this may require a separate analysis for each region or industry segment, the key in summarization is good judgment and prioritization. Regional analysis of the fringe benefits is an important consideration since each region within the United States may have dramatically different benefits. For example, the benefits package designed in Nashville, may be dramatically different from the one to be used in San Francisco. Optional benefits such as life insurance, and educational assistance at the locations should also be considered when completing a plan review.

Benefits in an international operation should be carefully analyzed on a country and regional basis. It is particularly important to review the details since each country may have dramatically different benefits required by law or local custom, and those benefits may be dramatically different than benefits that are required in the United States. Throughout Europe there are socially oriented countries that may require very different benefits compared to those in the United States. State, regional, and federal benefits may be mandatory, depending on the type of industry.

In all cases where the social and legal environments are dramatically different than those in the United States, it is important to obtain a qualified opinion and counsel to ensure that the compensation and benefits are reasonable in relation to the industry and region. While it may initially add a few dollars to the cost of an acquisition, a fair, unbiased review will be a sound basis to discuss benefits with employees in an acquired company, and it will be a good start to motivate the acquired organization immediately. If it is a new industry, benefits consultants should be engaged to review what is considered "customary fringe."

Once the baseline of the fringe benefits has been established for both the acquiring and the acquired company, a comparison should be made including the number of employees, potential cost, and type of coverage required. While it is possible to have benefits reductions in target companies, simply reducing existing benefits in a target will be difficult. You should consider a fair buyout in such situations, then a reduction to the acquirer's level.

Initial discussions with human resources representatives within each company should cover costs, number of employees, and transition planning, and timing. Once all benefits have been defined and potential costs have been estimated for the changes in benefits, it is important that these costs be reviewed and accepted by senior management.

NONMONETARY REWARDS

Creating a baseline of activity for both the acquiring and acquired company is the foundation for the analysis. The analysis should reflect the organization level of employees, the number of employees, and estimated costs for existing benefits. Proposed future benefits (such as extended life insurance, expense accounts, automobile allowances, and club dues) should be understood in the initial planning process. Integration timing and speed are critical. Move quickly and effectively, and stay on target for a quick transition.

During the review of the nonmonetary awards (e.g., internal promotional trips, recognition awards, performance clubs, and memberships), human resources representatives should carefully consider the sales awards, annual incentive trips, and honors given to the best-performing sales reps. Again, these employees are the primary contact with the outside—the customers. It is important to continue to reinforce the incentives that keep these employees motivated. As the sales incentives, trips, and honors are reviewed, consider how these motivate the individuals, and don't focus too heavily on the possible duplication of costs to have a dual reward system for the initial transition period.

Honor existing commitments, regardless of the difference from the buying company's plans, or you will lose the trust of the organization. Regaining the target company employees' trust will be very difficult if you don't acknowledge and deliver prior commitments in the near term. If a sales rep program includes a trip to Bermuda for achieving a 30% growth over the prior year, the commitment should be acknowledged and honored, even if the acquiring company does not have a similar program. An alternative to completing the trip, if such a perq is inconsistent with your policies, is to buy out (honor) the rep's performance for a fair settlement.

COMMUNICATIONS

Employee processes—those that personally affect the individual employees—are high-visibility and high-risk processes during any transition. Effective communication to employees should be complete, be timely, and include appropriate information. While there are many methods to communicate, it is important to understand that the written, video- or audio-taped, or Web-based communication will be most easily understood if well done, and also will be the least subject to misunderstanding by the employees.

The most formal communication process is written or on videotape, and it can be delivered in meetings (one on one or large), in memos, letters, policies, or brochures, or through the Internet. Real time is best when the communications channel is properly controlled. Although informal meetings provide a more personal approach, they increase the risk of miscommunication since they may not follow the scripted meeting agenda. Be careful in preparing for these open meetings, and anticipate questions to avoid miscommunication.

Question-and-answer sessions provide insight into the concerns of the employees. Summaries of the issues and the organizations asking the questions should be mapped to identify patterns or broad concerns about the transition. Questions and answers through an intranet or Internet provide a documented trail of issues—not to be used maliciously against the employees but to help guide the company's understanding of the organization. An intranet page allows for controlled responses to the questions, timely response to all employees, and a resource that can be accessed at any time. The intranet is an ideal business communication tool.

QUICK CHECK OF CHAPTER 6

✓ Payroll and compensation

✓ Document "as is"

✓ Plan "to be"

✓ Personnel performance reviews

✓ Employee benefits

✓ Nonmonetary rewards

7

Understand the Key Functions and Plan the Transition

It may seem unusual to postpone discussion of all of the business activities—manufacturing the products, developing new products, processing the invoices, and so on—until Chapter 7, but consider what has been discussed thus far. We have identified the infrastructure of the transition and the initial critical success factors. We have established the purpose of the combination and the high-performance teams to do the work, and have focused on people management issues: strategy, task definition, priorities, and communications. We have also ensured that the people's personal concerns have been resolved (they'll be paid, insured, and cared for), and they will be managed through a goal/checkpoint process.

Now we can establish a master plan for how we integrate each and every functional area that makes sense.

In order to effectively integrate an organization, it is important that both the buyer and seller have a mission statement or strategy. If one does not exist, the buyer should create a mission statement to provide a benchmark for the acquisition. Throughout the integration process itself, the buyer and seller should understand that the business would not be as efficient as when the businesses were separate. It has been estimated that up to 30 to 50 percent inefficiency occurs during any transition period. Consider Exhibit 7.1, when you evaluate the tradeoffs between incremental spending to accelerate the integration process versus overall cost savings.

General Electric and other very effective buyers have adopted a 100-day program for integration. Consider the benefit of having a tightly managed

EXHIBIT 7.1 Cumulative Costs for 12-Month Integration

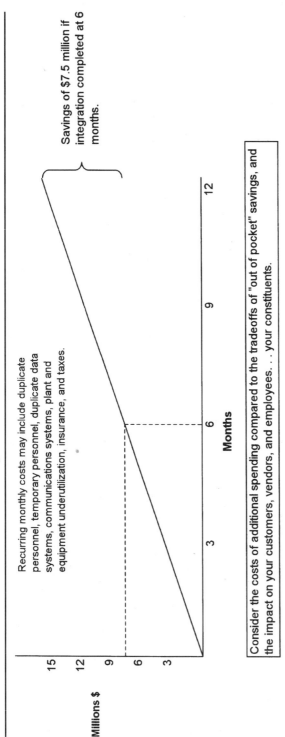

Recurring monthly costs may include duplicate personnel, temporary personnel, duplicate data systems, communications systems, plant and equipment underutilization, insurance, and taxes.

Savings of $7.5 million if integration completed at 6 months.

Millions $

Months

Consider the costs of additional spending compared to the tradeoffs of "out of pocket" savings, and the impact on your customers, vendors, and employees. . . your constituents.

plan with a fixed endpoint versus allowing the transition to be flexible without specific goals. If a company is purchased that has $100 million of sales per year and $50 million of annual organization cost incurred, a 30 percent inefficiency factor for a year will total nearly $15 million of lost efficiency—and who can calculate the impact on opportunity profit? Consider the expense savings, and the improved employee and customer goodwill if a well-managed, aggressive integration plan is executed. In this example, if the transition period is reduced to six months of inefficiency, savings will total $7.5 million. A properly managed integration plan will also more likely ensure an effective company integration and minimize the possibility of a failed integration.

A well-developed transition plan will prioritize critical processes in both operations based on input from executives in each business. The processes reviewed in this chapter will include those identified by Michael Porter in his book *Competitive Advantage: Creating and Sustaining Superior Performance*. Examples of the critical processes include primary and secondary activities, and cover functional areas such as infrastructure technology, inbound logistics, production, outbound logistics, sales and marketing, and after-sales support. It may be worthwhile for the reader to become familiar with these elements before any transition process is implemented.

Critical processes should be identified based on the strategic intent of the acquisition. Recall that strategic intent can include many reasons such as process improvement, establishing critical sales mass, and expanding sales portfolio or geographic expansion. As an example, R&D acquisitions may expand the near-term product pipeline to increase sales and possibly develop into synergy in the sales and marketing or manufacturing of the combined organizations. Strategic benefit may also result from an improved R&D process for future or unforeseen product development.

Each element of the business process will be considered in this chapter to ensure a reasonable understanding of the priority, timing, and planning required for the transition period. As you review the processes, you may find that an integration plan may not be appropriate. That is, a stand-alone or freestanding autonomous business may be the best result, considering the product lines, industry trade channels, employees, and countries involved.

Business process integration should consider processes completed (e.g., data systems installed and filed patents), the inventory of in-process projects (e.g., project status, investment thus far, and cost to complete), and the validity of the process itself (e.g., the international sales process is excellent). The initial valuation of a business should reflect an assessment of each functional area, prioritized based on the judgment of senior management and on available information. Although all activities should be considered to be effective, certain extreme performance levels may surface in the valuation—both favorable and unfavorable. For example, if a company does not have a history of bad debt write-offs, and days sales outstanding (DSO) are at forty days with no discounting, the buyer can assume in the initial valuation that the collection process is reasonable. This should be confirmed in the due diligence process.

Generally, all major new projects should be carefully assessed immediately upon the closing of the transaction. This could be an iterative process with quick preliminary approvals to avoid disrupting the business, but in the first thirty days, all major projects should receive a formal accept/reject decision.

DEFINE/ASSESS ESSENTIAL FUNCTIONS

In order to understand the keys to successful business integration, the company must define the strategic intent of the acquisition. The strategic intent should be defined in the valuation summary of the acquisition. It is important that the strategic priority of the function be determined because it will link directly with the mission statement or strategic intent of the acquisition. The strategy or strategic importance of each functional area will determine immediate tactical activities as well as strategic activities to serve as a foundation for the transition.

The strategic intent need not be precise but should highlight functional areas to emphasize during the integration plan.

The steps required to focus the transition team include:

1. Define the strategic intent for this acquisition.
2. Identify key related functional activities and areas to review.
3. Rank functions in importance to focus management attention and gain consensus.
4. Assess the target company competence. (*Note:* These assessments should be validated during the due diligence review.)

Senior managers should brainstorm all the functions and subfunctions within a target company and develop a master matrix similar to Exhibit 7.2 to assess the qualities of the target in relation to the requirements of the strategic intent. Primary functions may be expanded to include subfunctions to be sure that all target company functions have been properly analyzed. Subfunctions are the responsibility of the functional representative on the acquisition team and can be identified based on functional knowledge or information obtained during the due diligence review. Once the functional matrix is completed, the senior management group should evaluate critical areas in priority order. Weighting may be necessary, using a high-low ranking system or voting process (e.g., from 1 to 10) to identify the most significant functional areas. In the example, the weighting of the functions represents the estimates of six executives. Rankings identify the essential functional areas in the target company as considered in the valuation document or the strategic intent. This effort is not an onerous task but one

EXHIBIT 7.2 Due Diligence/Integration Reviewer's Guideline (Functional Assessment)

(1) Strategic Intent: Buy R&D process, personnel & strong future product pipeline.

(2) Description	(3) Ranking — Primary	Ranking — Secondary	(4) Target Company Assessment — Preliminary	Final
Research & Development	1		A	
Product Development Process		3		
Technology		2		
Personnel		1		
Intellectual Property		4		
Human Resources Development	6		B	
Administration				
Compensation Strategy				
Personnel Development				
Inbound Logistics	3		A	
Purchasing				
Inventory Handling				
Inbound Shipping				
Operations	4		A	
Production				
Outsourced				
Outbound Logistics	7		B	
Warehousing				
Shipping				
Sales & Marketing	3		C	
Dealer Support & Customer Service	5		C	
Infrastructure Activities	8		B	
Accounting		2		
Financial Planning		3		
Treasury		4		
Tax Planning		1		

Legend

(1) Always have a specific stated purpose for the acquisition.

(2) Note that the list of functions and rankings is consistent throughout the analysis.

(3) Preliminary assessment is done prior to any Due Diligence; final is a compilation of Due Diligence impressions and first impressions after the deal is closed.

Ranking is a task completed by each manager on the Due Diligence/Integration Team. Ranking of issues from one to ten will identify the functional priorities. As the numbers are summarized, the natural ranking or priorities will result.

Ranking is a hi-lo ranking of the priority of the activity as a strategic imperative or regarding its importance to the successful integration of the business. Subrankings will rank the activity within the overall Value Chain Activity. These will be finally determined by the responsible functional head.

In this example, it is obvious which activities are weak and which benefits and problems will be realized when the Target Company is acquired. Points of extremes (e.g. "A" versus "C") should be carefully investigated in the Preliminary and Final assessments.

that should be completed in no more than 3–4 hours of brainstorming to establish initial priorities. It is *not accuracy* that is important but rather *order of magnitude* of business risk or opportunity.

It is important to assess the competence or quality of the target company in each major subfunctional area. These rankings are qualitative assessments based on the management team's judgment on a relative scale compared to the buyer's competence.

These assessments will help to identify the opportunities that are considered part of the strategic intent and opportunities that are not critical to the deal but may present additional risk when the integration is complete. *It is important to assess these functions at a high level and not to become too involved in a detailed assessment. Judgment is the key. Only significant issues should be highlighted.*

In January 2002, Pepsi paid $14 billion for Quaker Oats Co. That deal no doubt included an extensive analysis of sales and cost synergies, and a review of the functional competencies of both organizations, and it concluded that the key to the success of the transaction was sales growth higher than the individual companies could achieve separately.

But to achieve that, Pepsi has decided to merge Quaker's sales-and-distribution channels into its ongoing businesses. It had not done that with prior acquisitions because all of its products had different distribution needs; syrup was sold in bulk to bottlers. Frito-Lay snacks were shipped by truck to retailers both large and small. And Tropicana beverages, acquired in 1998, used two methods—direct to the warehouses of chains and big users, and through distributors, to the small fry.

That last model was close enough to Gatorade to warrant combining it with Tropicana. Some Quaker food products will now also go on Frito-Lay trucks. With Pepsi sales staff hawking Quaker Oats goods and vice versa, Pepsi hopes to achieve cost savings while making brands an easier buy for retailers. "When you're dealing with the people who run Kroger and Wal-Mart stores, they're going to muscle you for every dollar."[32]

Areas at the extremes of the ranking may require additional review during the due diligence process to confirm the evaluation. At each stage of the acquisition and integration, executives will continually reevaluate their judgments to ensure a proper valuation and a well-planned integration process.

Note that the summary sheet also reflects the target company's competencies, ranked from "Best—A" to "Worst—C." When this information is summarized on a single page, the critical functional areas become obvious.

A process checklist may be used to assess the overall health of the target company processes. The checklist (see Exhibit 7.3) will allow the reviewer to consider each of the required review factors. As these checklists are prepared, feel free to add other salient information to the assessment. In the example, we've separated in-house and outsource as important information to understand.

EXHIBIT 7.3   Due Diligence/Integration Reviewer's Guideline (Blank)

	Expected		Final Assessment											
	Personnel Rating	Process Rating	Personnel		In-house Process					Outsourced Process				
			Performance	Capability	Documented	Verified	Assessment	Cost to Improve Capital	Expense	Documented	Verified	Assessment	Cost to Improve Capital	Expense
Description														
Research & Development														
Product Development Process														
Technology														
Personnel														
Intellectual Property														
Human Resources Development														
Administration														
Compensation Strategy														
Personnel Development														
Inbound Logistics														
Purchasing														
Inventory Handling														
Inbound Shipping														
Operations														
Production														
Outsourced														
Outbound Logistics														
Warehousing														
Shipping														
Sales & Marketing														
Dealer Support & Customer Service														
Infrastructure Activities														
Accounting														
Financial Planning														

Identify the critical areas in every deal, and allow for initial and final assessment. Also provide for cost to change to an acceptable standard, including both Capital Spending and Expenses.

LEGEND
A = Excellent
B = Acceptable
C = Needs Work

This second worksheet allows the reviewer to complete a macro assessment of the value of the individual processes compared to the established and implemented standard established by the buyer. *Processes should always be measured against the standards of the buying company.* The worksheet also provides a basis for estimating the cost to raise the level of the process to the desired standard—in other words, if the acquirers processes are best, how much will it cost to implement them? Or if the target company processes are best, how much will it cost to upgrade the acquirer? Look at this on a *macro basis* only—minutiae will delay the review process and not add any appreciable value.

Functional procedures analysis requires an assessment of the quality of procedures and a determination of their true application. Whenever possible, procedure manuals should be reviewed to assess the depth and quality of procedures. The functional reviewer should assess the quality of the procedures. If the documented procedures are adequate—that is, they meet the minimum standards established by the acquiring company—it is then necessary to determine if the procedures are effectively used. How often have we found well-documented processes that were never adequately implemented? Information sources that may be available for these assessments may include audit letters provided by independent CPAs (if available), internal audit reports, and monthly status reports. These assessments should be made during the due diligence process. If procedures at the target company are below the acquiring company's standard, an assessment of the cost to upgrade should be made.

The areas to be evaluated include all business functions outlined by Michael Porter and should include:

1. Firm infrastructure
2. Human resources management
3. Technology development
4. Procurement
5. Inbound logistics
6. Operations
7. Outbound logistics
8. Marketing and sales
9. Service

Areas that meet the standards established for the target require little adjustment. Those that are seriously deficient require a more thorough assessment. Plans to upgrade and integrate will be developed based on the extent of knowledge, personnel capabilities, and training required.

A complete integration may require changing personnel, establishing new processes, training, and the like. These should be carefully considered and planned.

INFRASTRUCTURE

Infrastructure includes general management, planning, finance, treasury, legal, and administration. These are secondary activities or functions supporting a properly functioning business. These functions may often be considered a lesser priority in a business combination, because the function does not develop, manufacture, sell, deliver, or service the product to the customer. However, maintaining a smoothly functioning process creates value.

Since infrastructure activities may be duplicated in the acquiring company or outsourced at the target (i.e., they may not represent core competencies), it is important to assess process quality and staffing.

The integration team leader and the team should prepare checklists of all significant functions, assets, and liabilities in each area for critical review and assessment. The checklist should be prepared and finalized within ten days of closing, and it should be updated to reflect new items. The checklist should include an assessment describing deviations from the desired procedures, policies, and controls. Specific areas of concern are listed below. As these areas are reviewed, look for narratives that discuss the issues, not just the numbers. Know your own company, including its processes and organization, and use this knowledge as a baseline checklist of all things to be considered for integration. For example, you know you have payroll, commission, pensions, and so on—chart these and ask the target company personnel about these or other related issues.

General Management and Planning

General management and planning processes concentrate on the performance and activities of the senior executive organization. The long-range success of the organization depends on the proper policies and on the implementation quality within these functional areas. General management responsibilities include strategic vision and the establishment of appropriate policies to guide the company to planned results. These responsibilities include planning with reasonable checkpoints to ensure that goals are achieved and an estimate of company resources necessary to achieve the goals. Definition of critical business indicators, report content, frequency, and audience are elements of successful management. The long-range success of the senior management team can be seen by its achievement of reasonably aggressive goals on schedule and within budget.

Reviewing results versus strategic plans, as well as budgets, can complete the review of these areas. High-quality ratings will be made when plans are routinely achieved.

Legal and Intellectual Property

Legal infrastructure includes not only litigation support and contract administration but also intellectual property for patents, copyrights, and so on and compliance with the required regulations and statutes affecting the business. During the past twenty-five years, intellectual property has become more important in the litigious global environment. Protection of intellectual property is critical in any business, which depends on improved products or processes. The effectiveness of intellectual property protection processes—whether completed in-house or by outside counsel—are essential when substantial investment is made in the R&D and new product development processes, since the intangible assets are of limited value without proper protection. If a substantial part of the valuation or strategic intent is to acquire intellectual property, the intellectual property protection and registration process should be thoroughly reviewed. This is important for all expected future products as well as those already developed, produced, and marketed. Consider the valuation if the team discovers that the patent process is generally inadequate or unsupportable. If this is a critical part of the strategic intent, for example, patented products and an extensive product pipeline, the inadequate process may be a "deal breaker." As the processes are reviewed, it is important that international implications be considered. For example, if geographic expansion is considered a likely result of the acquisition, international patent protection may be required. Will the past or existing processes withstand the requirements of the international patent process?[33]

Legal processes become more important if significant litigation is in process. Legal processes not only cover issues with customers and vendors but also may include those with government agencies and employees. During the due diligence process, specific attention should be focused on existing or pending litigation and on the processes in effect to manage the function. In addition, pending patent protection claims or claims in which the target company is the aggressor should be carefully reviewed to properly value the assets in question. All legal issues should be documented before deal closure to establish a benchmark for transition planning and also to assess the legal responsibility assumed in the acquisition. The list of issues may be included as a disclosure or scheduled item in the acquisition contract.

As part of any transition, it is important to understand, catalog, and prioritize all significant issues. Significant issues will be determined by the senior functional representative or outside specialist (and agreed to by the acquisition team leader). Once understood, prudent risk assessment can take place, and effective transition plans can be developed. For significant litigation and patent issues, it may be prudent to retain outside counsel to ensure that reasonable risk assessments have been made.

Summaries of all leases and existing contracts should be prepared and prioritized based on dollar commitment, risk, and the relationship to the strategic intent. Plot these items graphically to get a complete image of the target business—use symbols, colors, and graphics to better understand the integration issues that need resolution. The legal staff should identify business issues that may affect the successful integration to the ultimate strategic goal of the acquisition. Significant issues should be identified, and the individual reviewer must make a statement as to their validity in the functional area.

During the past five years, intangibles related to e-commerce have become increasingly important. Domain names such as WebMD.com or Amazon.com are unique and potentially valuable intangibles as companies market their products, services, and reputation globally. A thorough review of the company's e-commerce identifiers will ensure that the value of the assets is assured.

Finance and Treasury

The finance integration team must manage critical control areas such as cash, payroll, investments, and compliance with all debt requirements, government tax, and fiscal authorities. Finance and treasury operations are generally critical elements in any transition process due to the reporting and control provided and the cutoff issues encountered. Finance and treasury areas should be carefully reviewed during the due diligence process to ensure that reasonable, effective controls and reporting exist in the target company. *The quality of the financial information that is being reviewed is only as good as the quality of the process used to develop the financial statements.* If the internal controls are so weak that material misstatements can exist, financial summaries are of little value. Significant control weaknesses should be highlighted in audit letters when audited statements have been prepared. Experts may be required in insurance and treasury areas due to the type of exposure that may exist. For example, treasury is a function that may legitimately have transactions off the balance sheet, which may be disclosed only through monitoring interest expense and income, bank charges, and foreign exchange gains and losses. Recall that Volkswagen suffered substantial losses due to rogue investments by company representatives.

An effective finance infrastructure is necessary to properly manage a rapidly growing or broad-based business. In addition to completing initial transactions and records (such as sales invoices and checks) and creating an information flow of results, financial management should include establishing policies and procedures, and monitoring compliance. Initially, routine department activity—including details such as individual time cards, factory work orders, purchase orders, sales orders, or project management activity—may be disrupted by a partial disposition of a company. For example, if a division of General Electric is sold to Thompson Electronics, new data systems, timekeeping and shop floor systems, and business reporting may be required, since the data systems in place may not be available for sharing by Thompson. Be sure to thoroughly understand the initial record-keeping and reporting processes early in the negotiation process. Qualified personnel should assess the systems and processes (e.g., manufacturing for work order type or bill of material records) to accept the systems as usable and transferable after the deal is complete.

Cash/Debt Instruments

The treasury operations include not only deposits and assets but also debts, contingent liabilities, and financial instruments. Treasury operations are generally responsible for global financial asset management, monetary controls, and debt functions. Activities are not only limited to disbursements and collections but also include policies related to accounts payable, accounts receivable, and investment of cash available. These policies are the foundation of cash flow and cash balances. Policies will also include hedging and foreign currency exchange processes as well as risk management and insurance matters. Business process controls related to many of these "off the balance sheet" activities should be carefully reviewed. Processes should be documented if used, and thoroughly reviewed to ensure that the processes provide reasonable financial management controls.

Insurance

Insurance or risk management is often within the treasury responsibility due to its administrative process requirement and the significant benefit of "buying" power resulting from centralized treasury activities. Insurance or risk management is loss avoidance or containment. A complete review of all existing insurance contracts and risk management processes should be documented and reviewed with the treasurer or senior financial representative of the target company. Claims in process and procedures, to ensure that all pending claims have been documented, should be reviewed. For insurance matters, it is important to *understand risks that exist as well as those covered.* It is possible that in some small companies, senior management has assumed the uncovered risk of loss by not adequately insuring for the potential losses.

Consider the day-to-day business activity as well as strategic elements in the business. For example, if a company's strategy anticipates moving from basic generic pharmaceutical production to biotech products, the insurable risks may change dramatically. As the acquiring company modifies the business strategy, it is important that the company discuss the significant changes with the insurance carrier. These factors should be carefully considered, as such costs may be either exorbitant or uninsurable.

Insurance processes also should be reviewed as they relate to the amount of coverage. As companies change configuration, products, size, number and type of employees, locations, and basic processes, the companies may move among certain established risk pools. All business processes should be reviewed by the risk manager (internal or outsourced) to ensure that there are no undisclosed (hence uninsurable) processes or events. Examples of specific insurance coverage to be considered include "umbrella" coverage, product liability, general liability, foreign operations (i.e., FCIA insurance), directors and officers (D&O) insurance, and employee bonding. Coverage may exist and may be immediately available for the combined organization without additional cost with the simple addition of a policy endorsement. In the post–September 11 era, the business and insurance environment has become much more volatile. Coverage may be terminated or reduced as businesses combine to new risk profiles. All such coverage should be reviewed to determine the impact on the company's coverage and cost.

Workers' compensation in the United States is a cost that may be managed based on the size of the company and loss ratios. Investigate the kinds of risk pools—it may be appropriate to change declarations. In all cases, volume or economies of scale purchases may exist for a combined organization. Certain costs may not vary due to size of the risk covered and due to the "step-function" cost of insurance.

HUMAN RESOURCES ADMINISTRATION

Human resources policies and procedures are important elements of any transaction. All human resources (HR) policies and procedures should be reviewed for priority items as soon as possible—before completion of the transaction if possible. The transition team should consider organization, personnel, compensation and benefits, and human resources strategy. HR strategies require careful review to ensure compatibility with those of the buyer. If the strategies and policies are incompatible, plans to synchronize should be developed immediately to avoid a negative impact on morale—in both companies. The plan should be aggressively implemented and widely communicated.

Benefits strategy and specific plans for change of both primary (pension, 401k, health care, social security, and unemployment) and secondary benefits (tuition assistance, life insurance, and child care) should be developed to ensure that there are no gaps for all covered employees.

All significant human resources processes should be reviewed to determine if they are consistent with those of the acquiring company. Those procedures that are different or are inadequate require assessment, planning, and execution to change to an acceptable level.

TECHNOLOGY

Product Development

Product development is frequently a reason to acquire a company. Companies that excel at development, that have not been properly valued due to other business process failures, or that have been undervalued due to a lack of currently marketable products may find that they are takeover targets. Effective product development processes create significant future value, as has been seen in many analysts' valuations of companies in the biotech area and the recent consolidation of several pharmaceutical companies. In order to properly assess and integrate an R&D operation, the transition and due diligence teams should review the product development projects. Exhibit 7.4 displays a worksheet that concentrates on certain key elements of the analysis.

Technology projects will be continued, discontinued and sold, or discontinued and scrapped. The projects should be stratified or ranked by risk, trade channels product classifications, and their value to the new consolidated company. The reviewer may want to have a floor level of investment (e.g., only projects with cost of more than $100,000 will be reviewed) to prioritize the projects to avoid wasting time on less important projects. Those investments that do not meet the minimum criteria established should be scheduled for discontinuation or sale as soon as practical. Plans to discontinue should be carefully developed to ensure that the employee impact has been properly considered. The technology team leader should obtain approval that the projects are consistent with the strategy. Significant R&D project issues should be identified during the due diligence review. Once the acquisition is completed, high-priority projects or high potential sale value projects should rise to the top of any queue to ensure fast and effective disposition.

For those projects to be sold, the disposition plan should be the responsibility of a single individual who will coordinate the preparation of the prospectus as well as guide potential buyers through the purchase of the projects.

R&D projects may be easily planned and documented; however, the value to the company only occurs if the projects are completed on time and within budget. Review of documentation, the development process, and the project status is important in the due diligence process to ensure that, within a reasonable time, the process effectiveness has been determined. It is easy to prepare projections with estimated values, cost to complete, and milestones, but it may be difficult for an R&D department to actually manage to specific deadlines. Beware of continually slipping project deliverables. The flexibility in scheduling, number of changes to the target dates, and ability to meet initial objectives should be carefully reviewed to insure that the potential for the product is real. If the schedules are frequently changed due to missed deliverables, the future value of in-process projects may be doubtful. Areas of particular interest are the technical deliverables, the cost to complete, and the timing of the projects.

Technology: Communications Systems

Systems should be evaluated for sustainability, transferability, and compatibility with other systems. Effective communications systems are essential to a business in transition. An inventory of the essential elements of the existing systems—hardware and software—should be completed during

EXHIBIT 7.4   Research and Development Summary

Proj #	Strategy	Market Channel (1)	Sponsor	Description	Sunk	Cost To Complete (3)	Incremental Capital	Year 1 Sales	GM (4) Financials	First 3 Years' Sales	GM
									(Nearest $1.0 million)		
101	Continue	Consumer	Mkting	GPS handheld for cross-country	0.5	0.2	0.4	1.5	0.9	7	4.5

Legend

Project Number: An index number
Strategic Intent: Goal to maintain, expand or complement current line; or discontinue
Trade Channel: Describe the primary trade channel used
Sponsor: Person responsible for the success of the project
Description: General description of the product being developed
Sunk Cost: Cost already spent on the project
Cost to Complete: Total spending to bring the product to market
Incremental Capital: Required cost of manufacturing, sales, distribution, and so on to bring product to market
Financial: Sales/Gross Margin for periods indicated; may also consider Min/Max/Probable

(1) **Strategy:** This will be considered in an initial screening, and will either be within the strategic intent and be accepted, or be considered for disposal.

(2) **Market Trade Channel:** This is important to consider as projects are initially evaluated in the screening. This will also be a foundation for market planning and transition into existing Distribution Channels and markets.

(3) **Project Cost:** This is helpful to understand when evaluating companies and projects. Long-term, high-cost projects may not immediately fit the strategy of the acquisition. Sunk cost may be an indicator of "% complete" and could guide a saleable part of the research. Cost to complete is a judgment estimate - not necessarily a precise calculation.

(4) **Estimated Capital Cost:** This may provide information about future cash flow needs and refurbishment. Financials provide information to determine if the projects make sense for the combined company. In a small company, a $10 million product may be worth commercializing - in a large company, the effort may be too costly.

Note: Scale of investment, and not precision, is important in the development of the schedule. Consider the number and size of the projects as an indication of the management effectiveness—that is, if a $50 million company has fifty projects, they may be too out of control and diluted in their investment strategy to be effective.

the due diligence process. As essential systems are identified in the communications process, compatibility should be assessed and transition plans should be developed if appropriate. Consider that a sales force may be totally without direction if voice mail and e-mail were somehow disconnected or incompatible with supervisory organizations.

The systems that should be considered in this initial and final review include customer-facing and internal Web pages, telephone, voice mail, paging systems, cellular communications, e-mail systems, and compatibility of other support data systems such as Act (the sales contact manager) or Lotus Notes. *Take an inventory of all the support processes necessary to manage a function, identify those that are critical, then be sure that the systems will work in the future.* Critical systems should be identified and transition plans developed early in the due diligence process.

Technology: Data Systems, Hardware and Software

During the review, you should confirm the validity of software licenses used in the acquired company. This is important since some small companies may not strictly adhere to copyright laws—the number of licensed applications may be considerably less the number actually in use. In addition, as data systems are reviewed, company licenses may present an interesting cost-saving alternative. For example, if a larger company already has a companywide software license for an Oracle application, costs may be reduced once additional sites are added based on quantity discounts or block-user licenses; additional licenses may not be required. During any systems review, it is important to consider company licensing and not single-site licenses when initial contracts are being negotiated. The target company may have such licenses, or the acquiring company may have such agreements.

Data systems reflect the control elements or internal control reporting available for any business. Three review areas of the data systems should be considered:

- An assessment of the control environment
- An assessment of current operations by a functional area (i.e., communications, MIS, and Web applications)
- An assessment of the business strategy (as it relates to data systems and communication processes)

Technology: Data Systems Control Environment

The systems control environment allows an organization to function effectively by processing the correct information and using the appropriate system to provide accurate results. The control environment is the joint responsibility of the MIS department and the functional department establishing the initial record—for example, manufacturing, finance, sales, or marketing. The MIS department is responsible to provide a smoothly functioning process that provides an environment for timely, accurate processing of all data. This will include every system from the shop floor processing, to accounts payable, accounts receivable, sales and invoicing, inventory control, and so on. Each of these areas may be essential in the business—our priority areas.

Examples will include inbound logistics, production planning, inventory control, outbound logistics, and sales. Financial accounting and other data systems are support systems but are also critical to the success of the business.

The MIS representative should prepare a summary of all active data systems, stratified from high to low priority based on strategic intent and business risk. Other team members (manufacturing, finance, and so on) should confirm priority assessment. Once summarized, the systems should be reviewed to determine if a transition to the acquiring company systems is needed or if the target company systems are adequate and meet minimum standards established for the buyer. If not consistent with the buyer's requirements, time and cost estimates to upgrade to the buyer's standard should be prepared on a macro basis if necessary for later refinement.

Assessment of the hardware and software requirements for each organization should be documented as is, including what is expected. In each case, plans or upgrades that are in process should be documented to ensure that the company:

- Understands the current status of the plan and extent of the commitment
- Understands cost to complete
- Understands time to complete
- Understands consistency or compatibility with other systems

For those systems that have recently been approved and major expenditures have not been made, the project should be temporarily stopped to reassess continued spending. This factor should be considered in all major spending programs throughout the organization's functional areas.

Functional Assessment

A functional assessment should determine if the systems are compatible with the buyer's existing systems'. If not, an impact assessment should be developed to understand the complexity of change—time, cost, and disruption to business. The analysis should reflect the purpose of the acquisition and an assessment by the functional reps on the transition team.

Linkage of the data systems' requirements to the business strategy is very important. In a fast-growing business, the growth of the operation may be constrained by the low-quality system's installation. Well-designed data systems will complement the business strategy and not be a secondary activity. Well-designed systems strategies will provide the type of management control that fits the business. High-volume, small-dollar transaction business environments require different systems than high-dollar, less frequent sales functions. Systems strategies are developed based on an understanding of the breadth and depth of requirements. Systems strategy development, selection, and installation can require 6–12 months or can require many years for the more complex enterprise systems.

During the initial due diligence review, all team representatives should evaluate the systems. The assessment includes a review of the current installed system and its functionality, plans and strategies for future investment, and an assessment of the current MIS projects already in process or to be started. All major projects should be put on hold until a reasonable judgment can be made about their future usefulness.

PROCUREMENT AND INBOUND LOGISTICS

Inbound logistics reflect the activity with essential suppliers (e.g., labor, materials, and service contractors). All supplier relationships should be documented and summarized. Critical suppliers should be identified early in the due diligence process. Relationships with critical suppliers should reflect location, products supplied, critical nature to the company, and competitive or substitute products available. The relationships should be reviewed to determine whether the type of relationship is contractual or informal. This will allow the acquiring company to assess the risk related to the relationship and the cost to continue or cancel the relationship. Compatibility with the acquiring company may be assessed initially during the review. Exhibit 7.5 will show you an example of a supplier summary.

A spreadsheet may be used to allow for sorting among the many possible priorities. For example, using a high-low annual usage prioritization, sorting by location, and comparing to the acquiring company's own sourcing may disclose an unusual concentration of buying with a single source. In addition, by including approximate annual volume, the company may be able to negotiate additional volume discounts—immediately. Contractual relationships are important since the company may want to terminate or discontinue service with certain suppliers. Sorting by product may identify common product purchases—such as software—that would allow the company to deal with a more reliable company. The purchasing representative must use judgment and management skill to summarize enough information to manage a successful integration. Accuracy is not as important as order of magnitude and speed in this process. The individual will never be 100 percent accurate but will be able to develop a meaningful transition plan in a short time.

During the past decade, outsourcing of noncore processes has become a typical business practice. Significant outsourced activities or products

EXHIBIT 7.5 Supplier Summary

Type	Vendor Name	Alternate Suppliers	Longevity Past	Future	Locations Supplied	Products Supplied	Annual Volume (Millions $)
Contract	Johnson & Wesley	none	17	3	Chicago Detroit	Casting, Precision machined parts	4

Legend

Type: Contract or Informal
Name: Company Name
Alternate: Name Alternate source
Longevity: Historical relationship, and future contract commitment
Location: Locations served
Products supplied: Brief description for analysis
Annual volume: Estimated in Million of dollars

This analysis is meant to give the acquirer a picture of the sourcing profile used by the Target Company. Consider what is important to you and capture the information. This could lead to reduced costs, improved logistics relationships and improved quality. Also consider hi-lo analysis by product, supplier and location to identify those features that will have the greatest impact on the integration of the businesses.

should be summarized, including sufficient information to discuss with other team members. For example, circuit board assembly may be outsourced at the target company and may be easily assembled in the acquiring company. When such areas are identified, the functional representative that would be responsible inside the company after the merger should determine if the third-party relationship should continue.

It is important to consider the relationship and the impact on the total company when operations are combined. For example, the suppliers may provide quantity price breaks, multiple drop-ship areas, or more generous credit terms as a larger company with broader reach and higher volumes acquires a smaller company.

As the inbound logistics suppliers are identified—including not only tangible product suppliers but also intangible service suppliers (i.e., banks, processing services, and consultants)—the company should determine which logistics strategy meets the company's requirements. While this may seem like a simple statement, consider that the logistics strategy with essential suppliers may be dramatically different between the two companies. During the past five years, transportation companies have become critical elements of the logistics strategy. During the transition, it may be an ideal time to negotiate the existing logistics relationships and expand services.

As the inbound logistics are reviewed, upside and downside changes to existing relationships should be considered. These relationships include not only the target company relationships but also those of the parent company. Factors that may affect the transition activities include existing contracts, locations served, pricing, and credit terms. Each of these may be subject to renegotiations provided that a benefit can be realized from the logistics supplier.

Any integration plan should consider the immediate needs of the organization by providing a product and service to the manufacturing operation. Prioritized plans should be developed and coordinated with the inbound logistics groups from each location. The transition team member designated as responsible for inbound logistics must agree with the transition plans as well as contingency plans to ensure continued inbound logistics services.

Inbound logistics may also include inventory management, purchasing, and outsourcing strategies as are used by Dell Computer—where inbound logistics have been shifted to the freight carriers and the suppliers.

OPERATIONS

Production operations and facilities should be summarized on a worldwide basis for each company. Significant items should be summarized; these may vary by organization. The production summaries should include a designation of whether owned or leased. If leased, terms should be reviewed carefully to identify obligations and determine if there are any business risks related to the production facility. In addition to the owned/leased designation, each location should include a description of the type of operation and organization related to the production. See Exhibit 7.6.

Production operations are a primary activity in most companies. Transition of this activity requires careful management, since a misstep may disrupt customer service. The function requires a top-down, macro review and a comprehensive review of procedures if there is any intent to relocate processes or production operations.

Outsourcing should be reviewed carefully to ensure that conflicts within the combined companies are avoided. A thorough review of all processes should highlight critical outsourcing activities. In each case, production "know-how" should be reviewed to determine if the processes are adequately documented in essential areas. Manufacturing engineering specifications are often different that the final products produced due to minor "line changes."

Procedures/Strategy

Manufacturing procedures and production expertise may be critical elements in the acquisition. Production personnel must assess the documentation. A production team member should review the extent of documentation, procedural controls, and so on at the target companies. It may be difficult or impossible to review each location. However, if there are policies and procedures requiring compliance, there may be "audit" departments that ensure the procedures are followed. Quality assurance may review and report compliance for each location. If possible, reports from the QA organization should be obtained to determine the degree of compliance with existing procedures and policies. If it is expected that the processes will be transferred, a manufacturing representative must review the available processes and documentation to determine if they are adequately defined and may be successfully and reasonably transferred. If the manufacturing team member is responsible for continued operation of the acquired plant, they will make an informed decision that the facility operates to the standards equal to the acquiring company. Deviations from these standards should be raised to a policy level to ensure that there is no misunderstanding and to ensure that corrective action is taken.

Procedure review should include an understanding of manufacturing strategies. During the past ten years, the "just in time/synchronous flow" manufacturing philosophy has become a standard process for progressive companies. Manufacturing strategy may vary dramatically among companies, so reviewers should understand the significant strategy difference and the impact on procedures, and estimate the impact on the integration (time, resources, and total cost).

EXHIBIT 7.6   Facility Review: Operations/Production Summary

Description:	Description	Amount	Reference
	# Employees		
	# Shifts		
	% Capacity		
	Square Footage		
	Production		
	Distribution		
	Other		

Reference	Characteristics	Book Value ($.0 Millions)	Current Market	Headcount	% Capacity	Weighting	Rating (Hi of 5)	Discussion
	Circuits							
	Board Preparation			2		2	3	
	Populate			5		5	3	
	Test			1		2	3	
	Clean			1		3	3	
	Shell							
	Consumer 1			1		3	3	
	Consumer 2			1		3	3	
	Consumer 3			1		3	3	
	Consumer 4			1		5	2	
	Assembly							
	Consumer 1			1		3	3	
	Consumer 2,3			1		3	3	
	Consumer 4			22		5	2	
	Industrial 1			1		2	3	
	Industrial 2			2		4	3	
	Industrial 3			1		3	3	
	Departments - Indirect							
	Receiving			1		3	3	
	Inspection			1		3	3	
	Finance			3		3	3	
	Warehousing			4		3	3	
	TOTAL			50				
	Other:							

A standardized format for multiple locations tailored to your business will make the review and decision process much simpler and more effective.

Note: Consumer Product 4 is the most important, with the highest concentration of employees, and the worst rating for performance versus the buyer standard. This may indicate a need for product transfer or process improvement.

Production Facilities

After the production operation has been reviewed, consider four questions related to the physical assets. How much investment is required to:

- Upgrade systems to company standards?
- Maintain operations without expanding quality, capacity, or capabilities?
- Add capacity to meet the strategic requirements of the transaction?
- Properly dispose of the facilities?

The strategic manufacturing facilities requirements should be defined regardless of the existing components. Once planned, all facilities should

be reviewed to determine their fit within the strategy and their final disposition. The plan to invest, maintain, or dispose of facilities should include
approximate timelines and overall financial impact as it relates to the
initial acquisition. Disposition costs or losses to upgrade facilities to
minimum standards may be considered part of the acquisition cost, or a
one-time charge to write down the value of assets to represent the value to
the acquiring company. Be sure to prepare estimates since separate
accounting treatment may be available for these costs. It is important that
all facilities be compared to the acquiring company minimum standards
rather than to those simply desirable.

Assess Production Capabilities

When evaluating the transition, each manufacturing operation should be
considered as a separate investment decision.

For each, a facility continuation or discontinuation decision should be
made. Factors that will affect continued operation include:

- Physical facilities and required upgrades to existing facilities and maintenance
  status
- Labor status (union, nonunion, professional, administrative, and so on) including availability of appropriately skilled labor
- Labor force capacity to learn (e.g., upgrade to computer-controlled equipment
  may be beyond the learning capacity of some labor forces)
- Accessibility or remoteness to other company operations (e.g., a bulk plastic production facility in Houston may have a small benefit to a manufacturing operation in South Carolina)

All critical operations should be reviewed considering each of the above
items. A simple checklist, prepared by manufacturing representatives,
would include the following ratings:

- Equipment/facilities need repair (include an estimate)
- Acceptable for current technical activity
- Acceptable for strategic intent
- Excellent facilities

Capacity Utilization

These assessments should be done by those responsible for continuing operations. In addition to the facilities review, percent-of-capacity utilization for
the newly acquired and "to be" state should be documented. This need not be
an extensive analysis but rather an intuitive one based on production information available and local knowledge, which can be refined later. Short-term

and long-term production needs should be considered against the available capacity. The surge-capacity considerations should be reviewed, considering seasonal production requirements and the combined benefits for both companies. A benefit often included in the valuation of an acquisition is the "synergy" benefit of combined operations—generally quantifying either the excess capacity that will be trimmed or the reduced combined overhead. The manufacturing operations personnel should agree to the changes in concept and the dollar value of savings before they are assumed into any valuation. Excess capacity in the future may be a drag on earnings and potentially increase product cost when considering fully absorbed product cost.

Location

Geography is an important consideration in all acquisitions. Production in preferred countries may be useful to legally avoid or minimize import duties and taxes, but it also adds complexity to the coordination and management process. As the geography is reviewed, import duties, tax regulations, and available grants should be considered during the deal valuation. Be wary of required changes in management structure and process due to additional production facilities.

OUTBOUND LOGISTICS

As with inbound logistics, all relationships should be summarized and cataloged. Outbound logistics are a critical link to the customers and *should be considered a priority in almost any acquisition*. As current outbound logistics resources are compared in both companies, it is important that the logistics be evaluated as if this were a totally new investment decision. Evaluation of the services as if they were totally new will allow for an unbiased decision, which should maximize strategic value for the company. If, at the conclusion of the assessment, the target company's logistics process is better, the acquiring company should upgrade to the better process. It would be a mistake to assume that the acquirer always has a better process.

Recall that in the communications chapter (Chapter 4), we discussed that the customer is a constituent that will be affected by a transition. The transition plan should allow for—or require solicitation of—customer comments based on their expectations. The plan should also consider systems and process compatibility with important customers. Transition plans need not be rushed but rather must be carefully prepared to ensure that there are no adverse logistics problems. The transition plan should include timetables, individual responsibilities, and estimated costs. Such an all-encompassing transition plan must be reviewed and accepted by management from each operation.

SALES AND MARKETING (U.S. AND FOREIGN)

Sales and marketing organizations are the primary points of customer contact. All facets of the sales and marketing process should be assessed before a deal is completed. This, of course, includes sales strategy, policies, and procedures as well as organization and people.

Sales strategies should be initially assessed in the transition planning process. Depending on the business cycle and the products sold, the strategy may differ among companies. Sales strategies may focus heavily on new accounts, and little effort may be concentrated on maintaining existing accounts. Product sales cycles may differ due to product lines. Corporate systems, sales activity, promotion, and the management process may vary dramatically. The real question that must be answered is "How do you want to interact with your customer?" Sales summaries by channel type may be prepared to identify the existing and strategic channels in the combined company. The summary can be in dollars, sales orders, or ship-to information, or it can be prioritized based on overall gross contribution. Judgment is to be used by the functional leader. Consider some of the variables that exist among companies:

- "Hunter salespeople" who are compensated based on their ability to acquire new business
- "Farmer salespeople" who are compensated to maintain relationships with existing customers
- Sales support operations that are compensated to execute sales transactions to the customer's satisfaction
- Marketing organizations that are designed to understand, market, train, and to provide after-market support to the customers

It is important that seasoned sales and marketing specialists carefully assess the sales/marketing environments at each location to ensure that a fair evaluation of the essential strategies and tactical activities has been completed. In addition to these proactive areas, understanding market characteristics such as competitive products and "product failure" (in the eyes of the customer) are very important.

Each of these types of organizations requires different management skills. Management skills include understanding the individual drivers, reporting processes (both the formal and informal), and goal setting that are consistent with strategy and current-year tactical plans. Each of the organizations requires data, data systems support, and communications support.

Areas that also require careful review as the sales operations are blended together are product training and organization structure. This is critical since the sales representatives represent the company to all customers.

They are the image of the company. If they are confused or improperly trained, the customer may lose confidence in the combined company. Product compatibility, organization compatibility, training methods, and monitoring methods must be carefully reviewed.

Product marketing and planning are important considerations in the transition planning. Each company will have a defined marketing mix, or an allocation of resources that are designed to best represent the company and the products to the selected customer base. As the marketing is reviewed, the communications related to the product lines should be reviewed. Areas such as type of marketing communication (TV, radio, print, the Web), audience, frequency, budgets, and so on should be summarized and compared among the companies. The strategy for the combined company should be compared to the separate companies. Once the strategies are aligned, you should review the tactics that must be completed. This includes all points of contact with the designated customers (e-commerce, print, video) and purpose of contact (training, selling, and after-market support).

DEALER SUPPORT AND CUSTOMER SERVICE

Dealer support and customer service become critical in many companies. For example, Compaq Computer acquired Digital Equipment to obtain its dealer support, customer service, and training network. As such, this was a strategic priority for Compaq. Other areas that require continuous dealer support and customer service may include heavy equipment, data systems, telecom equipment companies, or medical equipment companies. It is important that this portion of the marketing be carefully reviewed to ensure that there are no significant differences. Executives responsible for these areas in both companies should review, analyze, plan, and execute the transition plan. The transition plan should consider many items that can be developed in a brainstorming session by the transition teams. Some examples of issues may include:

- Spare parts availability and distribution
- Product documentation
- Warranties
- Language requirements
- Training requirements
- Compatibility of product lines
- Customs declarations
- Packaging and designs

Customer Process and Marketing

In order to protect the value of the companies, both current and potential customers must be carefully managed. Disruption in customer service or customer communication will be viewed negatively and will create a major opportunity for your competitors. Studies show that it is easier and less expensive to keep a customer than to acquire one. The competitors will be predatory during the initial transition period: Dell increased promotion and effectively reduced selling prices through free shipping to gain advantage over Compaq during their acquisition of Hewlett-Packard. Missteps in these areas may cause part of the estimated 30–40 percent inefficiency or loss to the company. Sales and marketing executives should summarize major customers and markets and should develop plans to treat these customers very well. Tactics may include personal visits, personal notes and letters, improved customer support during the transition, and perhaps even a hotline. In the HP-Compaq merger, common customers may require a specific communications process to avoid any confusion.

Customers of the acquiring company may also require careful consideration. Separate communications processes should be considered for each customer classification. In the Compaq example, consider that Compaq has a high market share of private consumers and a high concentration of server users—small and large businesses. A communications plan for these customers may have two primary concentrations:

- Personal visits by tech representatives to business customers and advertising in business journals
- Media advertising for private consumers

Assume that competitors would take advantage of the disruption due to combining organizations. Preemptive communications processes should be developed during the due diligence review whenever appropriate. You may also complete a self-assessment of the market risk factors and preempt the competitors' attacks. Concentration of business with major customers on either side of the buy/sell transaction should be carefully reviewed. Pareto's Law should be considered: 80 percent of the benefit will require no more than 20 percent of the effort. Plans should be developed and ready for execution if the negative forces prevail.

Analyze existing relationships and broadly categorize by type of relationship, quality of customer, or other classifications that you consider significant to the analysis. Examples may include formal or informal as well as a rating of the quality of relationship: acceptable, unacceptable, or great. Significant deviations from the norm should be analyzed to determine why the relationships are either great or poor.

QUICK CHECK OF CHAPTER 7

✓ Identify critical success factors
✓ Use value chain master template
✓ Prioritize functions
✓ Define "as is" state
✓ Define "to be" state
✓ Develop transition plan

8

Product, Facilities, and Intangibles: Understand, Plan, and Execute

This chapter will discuss intangible (patents, trademarks, trade secrets, goodwill, and the like) and tangible (product, inventory, facilities, and other items) assets. In any business combination, it is important to understand both the tangible and intangible values acquired. Tangible assets are easiest to categorize, evaluate, and integrate into another business.

Intangibles, however, are more difficult to interpret, since they are not simply goodwill, brands, or the quality service images, but rather assets that represent an effective business image. In order to be successful, it is important to assess the images, which can include existing products and product lines, product types, and geographic presence within the market. The analysis requires that these various assets be compared with the existing portfolio of business image, a goal defined, and a plan to develop the ultimate "to be" state for the completed integration.

In each of these assessments, critical success factors should be identified to ensure focus and the prioritization of activity. In each case, a transition plan will be required that has measurable goals, timelines, costs, and benefits. Individuals should be assigned specific responsibilities. *But remember, it is important to prioritize and review only significant products and product lines.* Although we will discuss several specific areas, the process should be used for all tangible and intangible areas. Product can include the product itself, packaging, delivery, and product guarantees, and it may also include intangibles such as the quality of delivery, training by the sales and marketing force, order processing by the production and distribution

people, and even interaction with the customers by the finance department. The marketing function should coordinate the list of essential features and benefits of the product and the business image. Intangibles also
include rights, contracts, and registrations that the target company owns.
Intangibles may be, in fact, the foundation of the purchase valuation in the
future cash flow of the company.

Tangible assets include inventory, plant, and equipment, whether leased
or owned. As these items are reviewed—for example, identified, valued,
and assessed for the future "to be" state—it is important to think out of
the box and consider each significant asset as a separate purchase decision.
It is easy to value the assets at purchase price or appraised value. It is more
challenging to *explore value,* which requires that a seasoned manager be
challenged to review the assets acquired to improve value beyond the book
value or acquisition price.

As with all areas of valuation, due diligence, and integration, qualified
and seasoned managers should guide the activity. Acquisitions are the most
significant transactions completed by the company, so invest the right level
of management talent to capture the value. The actions required for all integration processes include understanding the unit operating environment,
the objectives of the acquisition, the overall company strategy, and the particular functional area being reviewed. Once the assessment is completed,
planning and execution will be critical. The following section highlights
some of the areas that are essential to effectively integrate an acquisition.

This chapter may present summaries or tabulation guidelines that can be
used to summarize product features. These need not be completed in full
detail, but the analytical process should be completed—that is, the
reviewer should consider the intangible components of the business. Rigid
summaries may not be required for any items except the most significant
product or feature in the company. Use judgment, and focus on priorities
and quick turnaround for the analysis.

PRODUCT

Product: Macro Definition

Products can include both tangible and intangible components. These
should be summarized and evaluated separately. All factors that affect the
customer's perception of the product and company should be categorized
and evaluated. The executive team, led by the marketing function, should
define all the elements of the broadly defined product—the business image.
Product attributes should be listed and ranked based on high-low importance
to the customer. The rankings should be from several different reference
points, which may include customers, suppliers, or an internal functional
driver. While customer and trade channels are easily defined, the functional
driver is less often used.

The functional driver is the critical value added within the organization—for example, the ability to manufacture high-quality, tight-tolerance micro-circuitry. The listing of the business attributes should be completed in a brainstorming session with key executives to ensure that all significant areas have been included. "Soft areas" such as high-quality training, a dress code when with customers, office environment, office picnics, type of stationery, and an advertising moral code should be listed, but please use judgment to avoid being consumed by the process. The list can be reduced based on a voting process similar to that which was discussed earlier. Perhaps the best index of product and business image is the value chain, which is a complete survey of all activities that affect the customer, product, and service. Once the summary is evaluated, judgment and prioritization should reduce the critical attributes to a reasonable number. In many organizations, these analyses exist for the buying company through policy and procedure manuals based on the strategic business requirements. While this is a more regimented process to define business image, it may be as simple as having an executive tour the facilities and create a list of changes that will be required (e.g., no casual dress code; uniforms must be used in the factory; and logos must be used on all correspondence). While these may be simple points, they may influence the market perception of the company.

Product: Micro Definition

The micro definition of product will include those areas directly related to the tangible product or service delivered to the customer. Exhibit 8.1 summarizes the most important features of the "GPS—global positioning satellite" device. Note that there are several categories evaluated in the listing. While technically there may be hundreds of categories, the marketing organization has prioritized these as the keys to success of marketing GPS devices. For ease of review, the summary is grouped into tangible and intangible sections.

The example reflects several marketing judgments that require experience. Without the capability to prioritize products and features within the competitive market, a valid assessment will be impossible. *If not completed in a disciplined manner, the analysis will be overwhelming and be of little value.* The analysis displayed estimates the value of the essential product at the target company—the GPS—against the buyer company and two competitors. These priority judgments are based on the customer's viewpoint rather than an insider's perceptions.

Features are the most significant areas as defined by the customer. Priority assessments relate to the importance defined by the customers. A rating of "5" is the most important feature expected by the customer. "Score" is the rating of each product as it relates to the individual feature. Weighted average value is the extension of the priority times the score. A natural prioritization will result from this quantitative exercise and will reflect the best

EXHIBIT 8.1   Key Product Comparison

Product Life Cycle Assessment

Product Description

Product Elements	Priority Assessment	Our Company		Competitors Target		Company A	
		Score	Weighted	Score	Weighted	Score	Weighted
Global Positioning Satellite - Handheld							
Tangible							
External Case - Dimensions	4	3	12	5	20	3	12
Watertightness	5	3	15	5	25	3	15
Weight	4	3	12	4	16	3	12
Impact Resistance	3	3	9	3	9	2	6
Battery Life	5	4	20	4	20	3	15
Compatibility with Panel-mounted	5	5	25	4	20	2	10
Intangible							
Order ease							
Phone	2	3	6	4	8	3	6
Web	4	3	12	4	16	3	12
Mail	1	3	3	4	4	3	3
Price	3	3	9	3	9	4	12
Credit							
Open Account	1	0	0	1	1	5	5
Credit Card	4	3	12	5	20	2	8
Delivery							
Overnight	1	3	3	5	5	3	3
5 Days	2	3	6	4	8	3	6
Warranty							
Term							
30 day Free	2	3	6	3	6	5	10
60 day Free	2	3	6	3	6	0	0
Extended Warranty	3	4	12	5	15	0	0
Replacement Parts	3	3	9	4	12	0	0
Training & Instruction	5	5	25	5	25	3	15
Service							
Regional Availability	5	3	15	5	25	3	15
Total			217		270		165

This kind of summary may be prepared for the key or critical products that are being purchased. The ideal summary will be prepared using broad estimates - precision in this analysis will result in wasted effort. Whenever possible, the products should be benchmarked against competitive products, including those of the acquiring company, if possible.

judgments of the management team. Groups as well as individuals can complete the exercise. As these features are identified, a competent management team will understand the underlying activity that creates the value. These values can be under the direct control of the company (i.e., manufacturing) or outsourced and indirectly controlled (i.e., shipping).

As the product features are prioritized, it is important to consider the features identified as priorities for the deal. In the example, the target company has particular strengths in Internet marketing and overnight delivery service. In any effective due diligence process, the investigators will determine the core strength that allows these strengths to exist and will develop a tentative plan to preserve or transfer the traits. For example, the Internet marketing may be the result of a technically astute MIS director rather than of marketing expertise. In that case, the key to the acquisition will be to guard the data systems function.

In addition, overnight delivery and replacement parts are identified as keys to the acquisition. Pursuit of these characteristics may lead to close relationships with key suppliers and shipping agents or perhaps excellent manufacturing control (JIT manufacturing and short cycle times). Identifying the root cause for the high ratings in this case may focus attention on the manufacturing personnel rather than on the company as a whole. A successful acquisition will preserve these critical traits.

Product will include the elements normally considered in the full product definition (product, price, distribution, and promotion). However, it is important that elements within these four components be prioritized to effectively combine businesses. Product, in its broadest sense, will include tangible and intangible elements. The product matrix should be developed for all of the primary products in each company. The matrix should include tangible and intangible elements. Intangible components will include sales support, delivery, and service such as a warranty. These product components should be summarized by *product line* and, when appropriate, by *geography*. It is important not to be distracted by creating a total list but rather to focus on essential product areas—that is, as defined in the strategic intent. Support products or byproducts can be discussed later.

Integrating the marketing strategy effectively is critical if a combined business is the objective. Marketing goals must be quickly integrated to avoid disrupting or disorienting the customer bases—the new and the old.

Price

Pricing consists of pricing strategy on a companywide basis, on a product line basis, and in individual product pricing. Define the objectives for all significant products in each business and group them by generic classification. Compare the product features on a pro forma basis to frame your analysis.

Pricing and margins should be carefully aligned to the business strategy for the individual units as well as for the combined unit. It is important that the pricing strategy be defined to avoid disrupting the current marketplace and confusing customers and potential customers as the company moves to the ultimate combined operation. For example, the product/pricing strategy can focus on premium product with premium pricing and full service. Market conditions and product position among the competitors will drive the pricing strategy. Remember, manufacturing cost may be affected by strategic changes resulting from the acquisition, such as plant closures, elimination of overhead, and reduced distribution costs. Changes in product cost should be factored into any forward analysis.

Distribution

Distribution should consider each element of contact with the customer. Product distribution is an essential element in any marketing plan. The review of distribution will include a definition of all the components of distribution and an assessment of the quality of each distribution element. Elements of distribution may be one of the last images of your product and company as it is delivered to the customer. Each element should be evaluated, considering the product strategy and market position. Elements of distribution may include the physical site, transportation mode, vendor, and warehousing facilities. These factors will be identified and evaluated by the marketing function in any comprehensive analysis.

Distribution should also consider all facets of location and quality of service in branch offices and affiliates, in person, by telephone, and by mail. It is important *to include distributors and agents* in the assessment of distribution to insure a total coverage assessment. As businesses are combined, business and legal relationships may be affected. It is possible that a combined operation will affect certain contractual obligations by country or trade channel, depending on the breadth and complexity of the business.

The distribution summary should include a matrix of all significant products (summarized by line) by distribution channel and major customers. Again, as with all other assessments, quality information and not just simple compilations of the issues are critical. The marketing representatives should use judgment to ensure that the analysis does not become overpowering and counterproductive. As the matrix is developed, assessment as to the quality of distribution at both companies should be prepared.

Distribution channels are extremely important when analyzing two businesses that will become a combined operation since distribution channels reflect the result of sales and marketing efforts among various outlets for the product. A careful assessment of the sales and marketing efforts—including review of the sales force type and quality and of the marketing efforts—will provide insight into these processes. This assessment can be quantitative as well as qualitative.

Tabulations such as Exhibit 8.2 will allow senior managers to validate any assumptions through review with other members of the team.

Trade channels are opportunities for synergy as well as focused effort. In some cases, the trade channels used by one company may provide a much stronger distribution channel for the other. Note the department store impact on the acquisition for the buyer. If not directly competing, the complementary product lines may have better sales and margins when

EXHIBIT 8.2 Review of Distribution Channels

Product	National Discounter		National		Department Stores Regional		Specialty		Distributors		International	
	Ours	Target	Ours	Target	Ours	Target	Ours	Target	Ours	Target	Ours	Target
Channel Effectiveness												
Household Products												
Gas Grill		B		C		(A)		(A)				
Charcoal Grill												
Firestarters												
Cigarette Lighters												
Industrial												
Propane Torches				(A)								
Propane Heaters												
Channel Sales												
Household Products												
Gas Grill	45	2	20	5	3	(12)	2	(12)				
Charcoal Grill												
Firestarters												
Cigarette Lighters												
Industrial												
Propane Torches			2	(20)	2		4					
Propane Heaters												

The above matrix can be prepared by the marketing representative and can reflect a qualitative assessment of Distribution effectiveness for both the Buyer Company and the Target Company. Ratings from A (Excellent) to C (Poor) can be used to define the assessment and create a "map" of the distribution effectiveness.

The circled areas indicate the reason for the acquisition - strength in the Department Store distribution channel. This kind of summary may also lead to reassessment of pricing strategy - Discount Chain distribution may not be consistent with the higher priced Department Store.

In the Industrial Product segment, note that Values (Millions $) have been used to summarize Trade Channel activity. These need not be precise but must represent reasonable values.

distribution is expanded to department stores. For example, the buyer in department stores is not distributing propane heaters, where the target company is strongest. Another form of summary is by dollar volume of sales, gross margin, or perhaps gross contribution. The key to summarization is to use judgment to obtain the best form of analysis and not to get mired in insignificant detail.

Promotion

Promotion includes all forms of communication with customers and potential customers. In addition to advertising and media exposure, promotion includes sales efforts, packaging, brochures, catalogs, and any written product disclosure.

Each of the businesses should be analyzed, summarizing themes used to promote product lines by region. These themes should be assessed for consistency throughout the product line. Promotion should be summarized in a format that reflects the critical elements of the promotional spending. Promotion "maps" (using shapes, values, and so on) or spreadsheets to define coverage may be appropriate.

Promotion review requires careful attention, since this is one of the pricing images presented to the customers. Whenever possible, summarize the promotion for the base company and the target company (see Exhibit 8.3 for an example summary). The summary may include the type of promotion (e.g., print, television, radio, or general PR), timing, products covered, and any other significant features that will assist in understanding the promotional priorities.

The summary should include enough detail to identify product image, spending patterns, and potential improvement goals to measure progress. As the details are summarized, develop plans to integrate the business to obtain the maximum benefit from the spending to meet the strategic goals. Sales representation should also be summarized. This should segregate sales efforts by type: direct sales, manufacturer's representative, distributor, Internet, mail order, and catalog. Geography, product lines, and trade channel may also be important to summarize.

Assessment of the Product Life Cycle

The assessment of all major products should consider the position in the product life cycle. Product life cycle (early development through mature product) assessment will allow for planning of the future products and identify future gaps in the line. During the assessment, you should consider the new product pipeline (refer to Chapter 4 for a description of the steps required).

EXHIBIT 8.3 Promotional Map

Description		January	February	March	April	May	June	July	August	September	Legend
						Month					
Radio											$ < $1,000
	Gas Grills										$$ < $10,000
	Propane Torches					$$					$$$ < $100,000
TV											
	Gas Grills						$$$	$$$	$$		
	Propane Torches							$$$	$	$$$	
Trade Show											
	Gas Grills			$$							
	Propane Torches						$$				
Newspapers											
	Gas Grills				$	$$					
	Propane Torches					$$					
Co-op Advertising											
	Gas Grills					$$	$$	$$		$$	
	Propane Torches										

Symbols can be used to indicate the relative size of the investment, but dollar values can also be used. It is also possible to display the Parent Company spending to determine spending patterns and possible buying leverage, or cost savings.

It is important to reassess the stage of the priority product within its life cycle, considering the combined product line. Products should be reviewed by product line and assessed as to their stage in the life cycle. This should be done for both the buying and the target companies. The assessment should consider the possibility of extended lives based on the combination of businesses. Based on the timing of the expected new product's introduction, products may be synchronized or coordinated among the two companies. For example, a short delay may provide an extraordinary benefit in the end, increasing the total value of the acquisition. Factors that should be assessed as they relate to primary products in the product life cycle can include:

- Development
- Introduction
- Growth
- Maturity
- Decline

Products should be assessed to determine if they are within the strategy of the combined business. Products in development or close to launch should be assessed to determine if they *should be introduced, given continued investment, or discontinued.* The analysis of developing products should be completed as if the product is a new proposal. Screening criteria should be applied to ensure that the product meets the strategic requirements.

Specific objectives may be established for the combined operation—hopefully to reflect synergy within the product area. Eventually, all products should be evaluated, and a disposition should be determined. If the disposition is to discontinue the product line, you may want to consider creating a plan to sell the lines.

FIXED ASSETS

The plant assessment will include the definition of the type of facility, whether it is owned or leased, and the kinds of activities that are completed in it (e.g., manufacturing, distribution, administration, product development, and/or sales). In addition, geography, staffing, and equipment status should be cataloged.

Exhibit 8.4 provides an example of a plant summary. A standardized format with characteristics that are important in the industry allows for an easy summary of all operations. These are generally judgment summaries describing the facility environment, including the surrounding community. The functional representative responsible for the location should prepare summaries for all locations.

EXHIBIT 8.4 Facility Review: Features Assessment

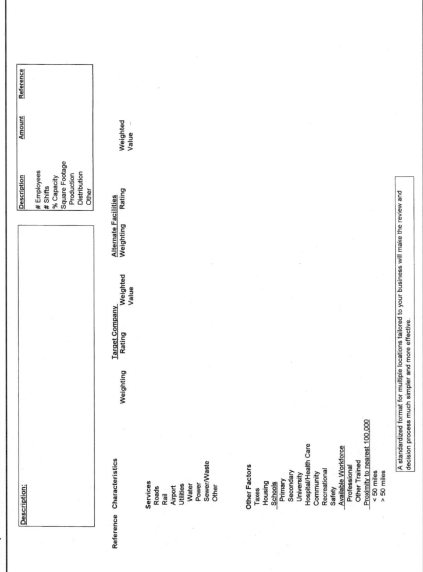

Description:

Reference	Characteristics	Weighting	Target Company		Alternate Facilities			Description	Amount	Reference
			Rating	Weighted Value	Weighting	Rating	Weighted Value	# Employees		
								# Shifts		
								% Capacity		
								Square Footage		
								Production		
								Distribution		
								Other		
	Services									
	Roads									
	Rail									
	Airport									
	Utilities									
	Water									
	Power									
	Sewer/Waste									
	Other									
	Other Factors									
	Taxes									
	Housing									
	Schools									
	Primary									
	Secondary									
	University									
	Hospital/Health Care									
	Community									
	Recreational									
	Safety									
	Available Workforce									
	Professional									
	Other Trained									
	Proximity to nearest 100,000									
	< 50 miles									
	> 50 miles									

A standardized format for multiple locations tailored to your business will make the review and decision process much simpler and more effective.

Facility Standards

Work standards in critical processes can be summarized by plant in a similar fashion (e.g., byproduct development standards, bill of material, manufacturing routers, department operations documentation, and/or workforce morale). Plant assessments should be done as all others are—with *preliminary assumptions* for initial deal structuring guidelines, *validation* through due diligence, *reassessment* if required, and *valuation change* if necessary.

As these facilities and related issues are documented, the representatives responsible for the integration should measure the organization effectiveness against the established standards for the combined company.

Significant investments to meet minimum standards for the combined operation should be summarized for each location. In the analysis, these should be summarized or grouped by type of facility (such as manufacturing, distribution, sales, and administrative). As groupings of these assets are compared among the companies being combined, it is important to consider the location of the facilities. Each major facility should be assessed as to the quality and serviceability of the operation, and compared to the minimum standards established for the combined "to be" corporation.

Manufacturing operations can include existing facilities as well as those under construction or major renovation. Significant process investments in any plant asset should be immediately assessed during the due diligence process on a preliminary basis as well as in a final assessment during the initial planning of the transition. Manufacturing investments as well as other tangible investments should be summarized as ones to hold, develop, or dispose.

This analysis can be completed using the same standards as the parent company or with new standards identified as the strategic requirement for the combined businesses. Major investments should be measured against customary or normal business investment criteria to determine the ultimate disposition. For example, the business standards should be consistent for size, quality, maintenance, and so on for all new facilities. Each acquired facility should be reviewed as a separate investment and measured as such. It is important that the same criteria that are used to assess each new asset acquisition by the buyer company are also used to evaluate assets acquired in a company acquisition. This consistent application of standards will ensure that the company strategy is kept intact.

Utilization and Core Competency

Manufacturing assets as well as other assets should be reviewed to consider utilization as an individual investment and as a combined business. It is important to consider the alternatives possible to potentially expand the synergy of the operation when the businesses are reviewed in total.

Manufacturing processes should be assessed and categorized *to identify core competency in each manufacturing location.* Core competencies can include electronic board assembly, chip insertion, tool making, and assembly operations. Each facility should be assessed on a macro basis to determine available capacity as well as type of process and utilization. Within each facility, if there are major concentrations of specific functions, these should be assessed individually within the building classification. Again, it is important to define the "optimum solution" for a combined operation when looking at tangible assets such as manufacturing, distribution, and sales branches. Once all assets have been categorized, it is important to make the decision to hold, invest, or dispose of the asset. Then the company should develop a transition plan. The transition plan may be a strategic and a tactical plan. The plan may take 5–10 years to implement or perhaps should be implemented immediately.

All facilities should be summarized by location and type of operation, and all significant factors should be considered. Factors such as organized labor, training, and impact on the local community should be considered in the analysis. As each facility is reviewed, *it is important to consider vendor contacts and contracts to determine if there are any critical or unusual services performed that are not reflected in the macro valuation of the facilities.* For example, local vendors may provide JIT manufacturing capabilities by scheduling deliveries hourly. This benefit may be lost in a combined operation that is moved to another city. It is important that the senior representative of each manufacturing facility be consulted to identify the major elements of the manufacturing process. Local management should be responsible to define the benefits (or sell the benefits) of the acquired facility to the buying company.

Outsourcing must be considered in each location since it can have a significant impact on cost as well as quality of service in certain areas. Proximity to overnight delivery, trucking, or rail/ocean port facilities may also be critical in certain product areas. Each of these factors should be documented and considered by the professionals responsible for the facility or function.

As each of these components of the manufacturing, distribution, or sales and marketing process is identified, it is important to understand the procedures used in the location and the transferability of the process.

Assess Production Needs

Production needs encompass both short-term and long-term requirements. To effectively judge the production capacities and expected needs, it is wise to examine synergy as well as product forecasts. Consider that new products in development at an acquired company may have a significant impact on the production facilities of the acquiring company. Short-term and long-range forecasts need not be precise but rather should give order of magnitude in sufficient detail to help the buyer company make a good judgment.

Geography is an important consideration as production needs are assessed. Proximity of production facilities and assembly facilities as well as proximity to customers and vendors should be considered before any combination decision is completed.

Disposition of Facilities

Each fixed asset has one of three ultimate decisions associated with it:

- Invest: Expand or improve the operation to improve the financial returns for the combined operation.
- Maintain: The operation meets existing performance and utilization standards, and it fits the strategy for the combined operation.
- Dispose: The asset does not meet nor will it meet the existing performance or utilization standards and therefore does not meet minimum strategic hurdles. Dispose/liquidate.

In each of these cases, the executive responsible for the functional area as well as the individual responsible for the fixed assets should assess the quality of the facility. Whether a facility requires substantial investment or not, the team must determine its long-term viability in the organization.

Geography

Geography is an important consideration, especially in an international organization. Many global companies have invested in substantial manufacturing facilities in Third World countries. Countries such as Mexico and China may provide reasonably sound investments; however, it may be difficult to effectively support a real-time or JIT manufacturing operation in these countries due to their limited infrastructure.

The geography analysis should consider physical as well as political risk and the proximity to customers and global transportation availability. Factors that will affect this assessment include quality of labor, training, facilities available, and infrastructure within the country. It is possible to have a high-quality operation in central-China but lack infrastructure such as adequately trained personnel to manage the facility. In 1998, Eastman Kodak invested heavily, in the education of workers who would staff their China ventures.[34] How could you possibly run an efficient organization if there were no trained personnel? In addition, as regions are reviewed, the current status of costly infrastructure and planned upgrades should be carefully considered. Plans may be easily prepared when compared to the difficulty and probability of successful implementation. When foreign investment and reliance on infrastructure improvements are critical (e.g., a hydropower plant in India), it is important to factor in contingency plans for long-term or permanent deferrals.

Leased/Owned

As facilities are reviewed, you should identify the status—leased versus owned—for all significant assets. Lease terms should be summarized and include significant features such as transferability, expenses, insurability, renewal terms, and buyout provisions. In certain situations, critical leases and their benefits may not be transferable, which seriously affects the suitability of the business.

INTANGIBLE ASSETS

Intangible assets include such things as goodwill, customer lists, copyrights, trademarks, trade names, and patents. These only have value if they have been properly protected, including proper registration in the legal domain in which the company operates.

As discussed in prior chapters, it is important to understand the business process in which certain assets have been created. It is of no value if a patent can be challenged and defeated due to an inadequate creation and filing process. In addition to reviewing the process, it is important to summarize the status of the existing intangible assets as well as any challenges that may exist. Written representations by target company executives and counsel are often used for this, as well as review by patent counsel, if the asset is significant. Regardless of the eventual legal enforceability of the asset, it is important to avoid the conflict through adequate due diligence review.

Trade secrets are an unusual intangible. These, by definition, have not been disclosed to third parties. The best-kept secret in the world may be the formula for Coca-Cola since this has never been patented to protect the formulation. The transition must provide for a proper transfer of trade-secret knowledge.

Registrations and Accreditation

Registrations and accreditations, such as ISO 9000, are important intangibles in any business. During the nineties, it became increasingly important to have credible statements about your business products and product lines. An innovation in that area is the International Standards Organization or ISO process. ISO 9000 represents a designation by an independent audit agency that a company or site has been qualified and meets certain process requirements. The ISO agency requires compliance on a periodic basis. Procedures must be developed to ensure adequate or proper production and distribution of products to comply with the ISO regulations.

Accreditation such as this should be reviewed to determine if the registrations are still in effect and approved. Those not in effect or abandoned should be reviewed to determine if there is any benefit to reestablishing the credential.

INSURANCE

Liability becomes an important part of any transaction due to the cutoff requirements at the transaction date but also because of the liability that may be assumed in acquisitions. Insurance can cover property, casualties, general and product liability, political or country risk, directors and officers, key employees, kidnapping, and workers' compensation. A business expert in insurance and risk management should carefully review each of these areas to ensure that conscious decisions are made and proper transition plans are developed, approved, and implemented.

The reviews should consider the amount and extent of coverage for each category, deductibles, umbrella coverage, and disallowed losses. As the companies are combined, it is important to recognize that coverage premiums may not necessarily increase in proportion to the change in perceived exposure due to synergies or buying leverage. Insurance represents an evaluation of risk probability, an amount of potential loss, and a profitability factor for the carrier. As such, pools are created and covered by the underwriter. A business selling gas grills will have a lower probability/risk assessment than one selling equipment for nuclear medicine. In addition, the pools may span a range of values. For example, a company with $100 million of sales may have a premium of $100,000 for product liability, while a combined company of $125 million may reflect no change in premium, although the sales are up by 25 percent. Work with a qualified insurance expert to understand the impact of changing product lines, geography, and personal risk pools to avoid surprises.

LEGAL AND REGULATORY FILINGS

It is important that regulatory filings have been properly completed. This is relatively simple in the United States, since there are standard filings that most businesspeople or qualified consultants understand. As the company expands beyond U.S. borders, however, there are unusual laws and regulations that by U.S. definition may not make sense but are nonetheless in effect. Experts in international law, taxes, and other regulatory matters should be consulted in an acquisition that involves these areas. Regulatory filings that have not been completed or properly filed may cause significant damage to the product line (products may be required to be recalled) or to the overall value of the acquisition itself. Major customers may be without your product because of your noncompliance with the regulatory requirements.

International or global operations bring totally new business risks and opportunities. It is not unusual to have contracts with agents or distributors throughout the world. In many countries, unusual legal status may be attributable to such contracts. It is possible that in certain Third World countries, multiple years' compensation will be required to cancel such contracts. Be wary of the unwritten and informal business relationships in the international environment.

Careful assessment of existing contracts and business relationships for distributors and agents is essential. These should be included as disclosures with any acquisition contract. Liabilities beyond established levels should be defined and assigned to a company in the acquisition contract.

QUICK CHECK OF CHAPTER 8

✓ Define "as is" and "to be" product

✓ Tangible product

✓ Price

✓ Promotion

✓ Distribution

✓ Transition plan

✓ Define "as is" and "to be" tangible assets

✓ Assess standards/practices

✓ Transition plan

Appendix: Due Diligence Checklist

This review checklist is an example that will provide a summary of issues to be reviewed during the due diligence process for an acquisition. The purpose is to assure that all material items that may have a potential impact either on the valuation of the proposed acquisition or on the future operation/integration have been considered. The guideline will provide *a foundation for reviewing* an acquisition, but *this should not be considered a total review.* Each acquisition must be approached independently, and therefore the reviewers' judgment and program modifications may be required. Independent experts may be engaged to assist in the review. Again, their judgment should modify steps or add review points based on the priorities, investment levels, and business risks.

The objectives of the due diligence review are

1. to determine an effective valuation of the target company;
2. to identify significant upsides and downsides to the transaction, and
3. to identify issues that may affect the successful completion of the transaction (including integration if appropriate). This includes a review of business processes and an evaluation of how they will be integrated with those of the buyer company. If the company is not at least at the buyer's standard of performance, estimates of cost to improve are essential.

This checklist is designed to provide insight into *not only the tangible portion* of the business acquired but *also the effectiveness of its business process*—that is, how effectively it works.

ACQUISITION DUE DILIGENCE REVIEW PLANNING

The acquisition structure and strategic intent must be understood. The reviewer should summarize such items as:

- Acquisition candidate prospectus
- Acquisition information submitted to the executive review team
- Draft copies of the letter of intent and purchase agreement draft
- Any available information that will assist the reviewer in understanding the acquisition

Once the team understands the acquisition proposal and main issues of the target company, objectives of the due diligence review should be summarized and prioritized. High-priority objectives that are potential deal-breakers should be reviewed with the entire team. The team leader will allocate or assign responsibilities among the team members based on their functional expertise. All segments of the business process (i.e., the value chain as described by Michael Porter) must be considered in the due diligence review. That does not mean, however, that a complete review of each activity is required. The team leader may determine that risk/opportunity are limited and eliminate the review of certain functions. That is the main reason for using seasoned executives in the review process.

Certain segments of the review may require experts that are not available within the corporation:

- Tax and legal
- Marketing
- Manufacturing
- Research and development
- Human resources
- Finance

The team leader must use any resource necessary to conclude a successful due diligence review. Outside consultants are very expensive, but reputable consultants may save a company millions of dollars of opportunity cost for a relatively small charge. It is important that the *value* of the review be carefully considered—if the company is spending $100 million, the review should be thorough. This review and questions asked of the target company management will be the bases for valuation of the acquisition. Although representation will be obtained from senior managers of the company, early warnings of risks and opportunities assist in the negotiation process. Experts are invaluable during an investigation of millions of dollars. Judgment is critical in the review process. Although the checklist is intended to be complete, it is not a substitute for each team member's dedicated thinking about the business to be evaluated. Observation of the quality of the people and the business process is essential for a good review.

Due diligence may require review of secret, critical competitive information. Nondisclosure or confidentiality agreements may be required. The target company, however, may still be reluctant to divulge the information until the deal is virtually complete. Reviewers must ensure that all workpapers are effectively controlled should the deal collapse. Generally, strict nondisclosure requirements, negotiated in the preliminary letter of intent, will require that all originals, copies, and other confidential information obtained during the due diligence process must be returned should the deal be aborted.

General Questions

Review the following with responsible management:

- Review corporate charters.
- Review bylaws.
- Review minute books and other corporate records to identify any significant business issues.
- Determine if the stock is validly issued, fully paid, and nonassessable.
- Summarize outstanding stock options, and determine if warrants or the rights to purchase stock exist.
- Determine if restrictions exist on transfer shares.
- Summarize provisions of bonus plans, employment agreements, and employee confidentiality or invention assignment agreements.
- Summarize key features of profit-sharing plans, pension plans, and other fringe benefit plans such as life insurance and major medical coverages.
- Summarize union contracts.
- Review any major or long-term commitments.
- Review any other operating details of significance that should be considered in the valuation or integration of the operation.
- Review significant correspondence from outside counsel in response to litigation letters.
- If a broker is involved in the acquisition, determine that the name and a proof of authority to act are correct, and review the agency commitment of the broker.
- If applicable, review the written brokerage agreement to identify all special terms and who signed on behalf of the broker.
- If applicable, who pays the broker's commission? Will there be an indemnification against brokerage claims?

The following sections present an in-depth summary of questions and issues that should be considered before completion of the due diligence review.

General Financial Information

- What accounting policy changes related to revenue recognition, capitalization, depreciation expense recognition, and so on have occurred in the past two years?
- Have there been any significant changes in planned capital expenditures?
- Have there been any significant disposals or transfers of assets during the past twelve months?
- Have there been any major changes in production processing schedules, quality control, or inspection procedures in the past twelve months?
- Have there been any significant changes in vendors or suppliers for essential components in the production process?
- Have there been any major changes in distribution channels or major customers during the past twelve months? Are there any threatened changes in distribution channels or customers? This must consider international as well as U.S. operations.
- Have there been any significant increases or discharges of security interests affecting assets that were not considered liabilities?
- Has the company waived any substantial rights of value during the past year?
- Have there been any significant increases or decreases in wages, bonuses, commissions, and the like of employees or representatives that would have a significant impact on the financial performance of the company?
- Describe any new employment contracts entered into during the last twelve months.
- Describe any significant loans or compensation changes to affiliated firms, corporations, entities, or stockholders during the past year.
- Have there been any changes in the dividend policies or stock transactions during the past year?
- Have there been any "favorable contracts" negotiated during the past year?
- Have any major business segments been discontinued in the recent past?
- Describe any significant changes in budgeted or plant performance—are sales spending, production, or capital spending during the last year significantly different than planned?
- Review available workpapers from public accountants for the most recent audit or business review. If available, review the most recent year's internal audit schedule, completed reports, and draft audit reports. Note any items of significance for follow-up.
- Review the most recent balance sheet, income statements, and business narratives discussing performance versus budget and prior year. Identify and summarize significant issues for other team participants.
- Obtain a list of the facilities and a description of activities that occur at each location. The list of facilities should include financial information where appropriate.

Examples of financial information would include sales, number of employees, payroll, total capital spending, products produced, and product development.

- Obtain lists of the largest suppliers and customers, and any projections for future purchases or sales. Identify the *sole source suppliers,* if any, wherever possible.

- Obtain copies of procedures and policy manuals. Review the following areas for financial or negotiation implications:

Inventories

Accounts receivable

Depreciation and amortization

Reserves and capitalization

Policies for revenue recognition, and evidence of their consistent application

Accounts Receivable

- Review the accounts receivable aging in total. Identify significant customer accounts and long-overdue accounts to discuss with management. Review credit department procedures in relation to the sales and receivables. Consider if procedures are adequate.

- Review credit reports and credit files to determine if procedures are reasonably followed. Determine the adequacy of bad debt reserves.

- Review reconciliation of the detailed accounts to the general ledger.

- Determine how accounts receivable are aged in relation to policies and procedures. Determine consistency with the company's procedures.

- Review historical bad debt and writedowns to determine if they are significant and if there are policy/procedure weaknesses.

- Describe the bad debt writeoff policy. Is the policy consistent with that of the buyer company?

- Determine if accounts receivable are pledged, factored, or otherwise restricted. Companies occasionally use accounts receivable as collateral for short term working capital needs.

- Describe the procedures to ensure that effective policies are implemented related to stop shipments, COD orders, and partial or advance payments required.

- Review Days Sales Outstanding calculations for the previous twelve months, identifying any significant cyclical trends (to be used for cash flow forecasting) or if the method has been applied consistently.

- Review the receivables including loans to employees and shareholders, unbilled receivables, nontrade receivables, and notes receivable. Significant accounts should be reviewed to determine if they are collectable.

- Review credit balances in accounts receivable, and credit memos issued to determine compliance with procedures. Identify any significant trends in the credit memos, and bring them to the team leader's attention.

- Review interest charges, cash discount policies, and their effectiveness. Determine if any significant deviations exist.

Inventory and Cost Accounting

- Identify the major product lines carried in inventory and, for the most recent year, their respective annual sales volume, normal gross margin percentage, units produced, and unit costs. Review for issues.

- Review the comparative components of inventory including raw materials, works in process, finished goods, demos, subcontractors, spare parts, and other. Balances should be reviewed over a reasonable period to determine if any unusual activity has occurred.

- Review obsolescence and the shortage reserves in relation to the inventory balances. Review consistency with the prior year to determine if any significant trends exist.

- Review the comparative elements of work in process and finished goods inventory. Observe trends and determine if there are any significant issues in inventory.

- Describe the inventory cost method. Review variances and significant charges in cost of sales to determine if there are any trends.

- If a standard cost system is used, describe the process for determining standards. Review with appropriate personnel to determine if the methods are actually employed.

- Describe frequency of review and content of standards. Determine if the standards are consistently applied with those of the buyer company. Are bills of material and routings reviewed periodically? Describe.

- Describe the principal manufacturing variances that are included in materials, labor, and overhead. Determine if these are properly stated in relation to standards and costs incurred.

- Review manufacturing variances to identify any significant trends.

Physical Inventories

- Review the physical inventory controls and book-to-physical adjustments. Determine if there are any significant issues.

- Determine if there are any significant inventory shortages, increases, or write-downs during the past few years. Identify trends and discuss management procedure with proper individuals.

- Determine if inventories are managed considering budgets, plans, and customer orders. What impact if any would advanced management techniques such as JIT manufacturing have on the inventory levels? Describe the opportunity.

Fixed Assets

- Property plant and equipment. Review policies and procedures for property plant and equipment including minimum capitalization levels, depreciation methods, useful lives, and disposal procedures. Review actual compliance to determine if a significant deviation exits.

- Prioritize investments over the years to focus on significant investment patterns. Compare investments by year to budgets or plans to determine if planning is unreasonable or valid.

- Obtain the current capital budgets for the company to identify any significant essential investments.

- Consider inspecting significant plants or investments in capital to determine if reasonable.

- Identify any items to be excluded from the sale transaction. All items that are leased should be identified.

- Discuss the facilities with local management to determine if there are any significant capital or repair bills expected in the near future. Obtain representations when possible.

- Review the construction-in-progress cost to determine if appropriate. Determine if project production in process is reasonably consistent with the approvals.

- When possible, obtain recent fair market appraisals of equipment and property to determine if purchase accounting is appropriate.

Capitalized Costs

- Obtain the company policy for capitalized costs to determine if it is within GAAP (Generally Accepted Accounting Principles). Costs should consider R&D, capitalized cost of data systems, deferred costs for major advertising and marketing programs, and the like.

- Determine if any capitalized costs require adjustment for purchase. For example, abandoned R&D projects must be written off.

Warranty Obligations

- Obtain copies of the company's policies and procedures related to product sales, service, and warranty.

- Determine if accounting procedures are properly described and executed to ensure that reasonable costs have been reserved for these obligations.

- Determine if there are any significant trends in warranty or adjustments related to product sales. Identify trends and obtain representations from company personnel as to their validity.

- Review warranty reserves and other sales reserves to determine if they are appropriate and consistently applied in compliance with company policy.

- Review the quality control deviations to determine if there are significant deviations from production standard.

Sales Policies

- Describe the company's policy for revenue recognition and determine if it complies with GAAP. Describe major distribution channels used by the company and a method of entering deals with dealers, distributors, sales reps, and so on.

- Obtain master agreements or individual agreements for major customers or dealers that sell the products to determine if terms are reasonable and consistent with those of the buyer company.

- Review pricing policies and procedures to determine the extent of review and profitability. Determine if pricing is within regulation—that is, if price preferences are economically justified.

- Identify return and exchange privileges. Determine if they are in effect. Identify any significant trends over the past year to determine if there are business issues that must be considered.

- Does the company consider floor-plan arrangements, repurchase agreements, or bill and hold orders in its sales process? If so, document and review significant issues.

- Identify billing procedures for freight and other charges. Are these consistent with those of the buyer company?

- Does the company enforce sales return procedures? Are proper approvals obtained? Are proper accruals made to reflect expected business exposure?

Contracts, Commitments, and Contingent Liabilities

- Review contract and sales commitment procedures to determine if they are reasonable and complied with. Factors to be considered include acceptance of purchase orders and sales orders from customers, government contracting procedures, and special or unusual deals with dealers and distributors. Determine if there is any pending or threatened litigation related to sales contracts.

- Review significant contracts to determine if there are any potential risks or opportunities. Consider that contracts may have exclusive territories and products that may conflict with those of the buyer company. Determine if contracts can be reasonably assigned. It is advisable to have an attorney review the master contracts as well as any significant unusual contracts. It is essential that international obligations be carefully reviewed due to the extent of liability often incurred in less developed countries.

- Determine if current liabilities have been properly reflected for purchases, services for contracts, and so on. Review the benefits accruals for accounts such as pension, workers' compensation, bonuses, vacation pay, and commissions.

Treasury

- Describe cash and investments as of the most recent balance sheet date. Determine if there any unusual obligations related to these items, such as pledged assets or security interests.

- Review controls related to investments or hedging for currency transactions to determine if they are reasonable. Assure yourself of compliance with these procedures. Determine if the valuation is reasonable and consistent with company policy and GAAP.

- Determine if cash flow forecasts are prepared and are reasonable. Identify significant changes in forecast to identify business trends.

- Obtain a schedule of long-term debt and nonbusiness debt by the company. Determine if the debtor interest rate provisions, restrictive covenants, and so on provide any unusual features that should be considered in the acquisition process or if they require changed controls during the integration process.

- Determine the extent and quality of existing insurance policies. These should include carrier name, policy number, type of coverage, limits, annual payments, and premium payments that are deductible. Determine if this is consistent with the buyer company's risk tolerance. Determine if there have been any significant losses or claims during the past year, and if so determine the primary causes.

- Determine if there are any hedging, forward-purchase, currency, or commodity contracts or any factoring agreements in effect. Determine if these comply with procedures and valuation.

Taxation: Federal, State, Local, and International

- Review recent tax returns to determine if there are any significant unusual features which should be considered in the negotiation.

- Review the latest available revenue agent reports on examinations of tax returns for prior years. Determine if there are any significant issues to be discussed in the negotiation. Review any available operating-loss carry-forwards, expiration dates, and unusual conditions related to tax credits, contributions, or tax-loss carry-forwards.

- Review the structure of the proposed acquisition to determine the tax status. Determine if the transaction is optimized from a tax and cash-flow viewpoints.

- Determine if there are any adverse adjustments or changes that would result from a change in ownership.

Legal and Intellectual Property

- Determine if there is any potential litigation or existing litigation against the company. Assess the valuation or potential losses and the insurance coverage. This should consider local management and in-house and outside counsel. Estimates of potential litigation costs and reserve requirements should be considered in the negotiation process.

- Intellectual property should be reviewed to determine if it is properly protected. Procedures should be reviewed with responsible management to ensure they are reasonable as well as fully implemented.

- Obtain copies of patents and applications, registered trademarks, copyrights, and license and royalty agreements. In addition, review master agreements and significant unusual agreements related to noncompetitive, confidentiality, invention assignment, trade secrets of significant products, as well as invention disclosures. Ensure that proper title exists for items valued in the balance sheet.

- Review with local attorneys, as well as senior management, to determine if there are any antitrust violations or FTC proceedings and U.S. Justice Department complaints.

- Consider the impact of the acquisition on these existing conditions as well as on potential activities that may be required upon completion of the deal.

Other matters, which should be reviewed during the due diligence review process, include the following.

Marketing

- Obtain and review the company marketing policies including pricing, promotion, returns, sales, warranties, and terms. Determine the process of how, by whom, and when prices are revised.

- Describe the stability of the price structure and unusual discounts or reductions in price compared to plan. Obtain a current outlook for the market of all major products and for expected significant future products.

- Review the sales force training programs, policies, and procedures. Evaluate these to determine if effective or reasonable controls exist for pricing, delivery, quality review, credit check in financing, post-purchase service installation, and product customization. Determine if there are any contingent commitments for advertising, product literature, support, training, and so on related to the sales role.

- Assess the sales planning and sales management functions. Consider review of the actual performance versus plans, budgets, and goals. Are goals established so that full compensation for sales employees is reasonable?

- Is there a process to obtain customer comments related to the sales/marketing programs and product quality? Determine if the company complies with the price discrimination provisions of the Robinson Patmon Act. This could be done through representations by senior sales management and the legal staff.

Product Lines

- Describe the major products and product lines that contribute most to sales and profitability today and are expected to in the future. Assess, if possible, the status of the product life cycle or the remaining useful life of each of the significant products.

- Review and list major products.

- Evaluate product strengths and weaknesses in relation to competitive products. This can be done by discussion with sales and marketing personnel. The extent of their knowledge should demonstrate their effectiveness. Determine if the current products have any potential byproducts or related products. Is there synergy with the buyer company's product line? Assess the applicability of or transferability of the acquired company's products to yours.

- Are there any potentially obsolete products? Determine by discussion and review of performance data.

- Review market share by product line, if available, and versus projections for future periods. Are there major differences? Can these be reasonably explained by senior management, or are they without information?

- Obtain copies of any market research studies or industry studies related to potential growth opportunities and market direction. Also obtain representations from senior management about the quality of its products line, the future of the products, and so on.

Research and Development

- Does the acquired company manage the R&D process considering prioritization of future value? Review actual performance versus expectations for the last 12–18 months to determine if reasonable performance versus expectation was achieved. If not, obtain explanations from the R&D senior management.

- Does the company use outside technical support in its R&D process? If so, has it taken reasonable precautions to obtain title to all outside developments?

- Has the company developed working relationships with universities or nonprofit government agencies? If yes, contracts should be reviewed to ensure proper title would pass to the buyer company. Are there any such contracts in place? If so, are relationships reasonable?

Information Systems

The MIS function is generally a critical support function in any organization. The company should be reviewed to determine the effectiveness of the MIS operations. This can be done based on project status reports, estimated spending in relation to prior years, review of technical competency, and personnel turnover.

- Describe the operating environment of the data processing department in all significant areas. You may find that distributed processing is used or a central processing system and a single location will be the control environment. It is essential that a description of the hardware and software installation be obtained. As individual members of the due diligence review team meet with management, they should constantly be aware of MIS control and effectiveness issues.

- The hardware systems and communication process should be reviewed to determine if they are reasonably protected. Procedures to safeguard the data systems are essential. Features such as fire control processes, hacker and virus safeguards, as well as backup and off-site hot sites should be considered in disaster recovery plans. Are disaster recovery plans in effect? If yes, have they been reasonably tested in the recent past?

- Obtain a description of significant applications processed in the electornic data processing (EDP) environment. These can include financial (such as accounting, reporting, and financial analysis), operational reports (job work orders and reports in the factory area) as well as marketing, sales, order entry, and customer reports used by the sales service organizations.

- All significant applications should be described with an assessment of their capability. The age, content, and ability to handle business in the future should be considered. It is also important to obtain an assessment of the potential, if necessary, to migrate data to the buyer company's systems.

- Describe the personnel managing the data processing function. This should include a complete organization chart and the employee profile within the company: education level, technical training, specialties, salary profile, and so on.

- If the company uses outsourcing, contracts and conditions should be reviewed to determine if they are reasonable and transferable. Contracts for outside services such as software upgrades, hardware support, and warranty service should be reviewed and documented. These represent major potential exposures should there be a disaster.

Human Resources

Human resources has two primary functions:

1. The administration of all personnel, human resource benefits, compensation, and commission programs.
2. The effective management of the human resources pool in the company. This would include an assessment of organizational requirements, training requirements, and the like.

The human resources department must effectively develop and manage the human resources—or people—in the company.

- Obtain a listing of all open requisitions. Determine if they are necessary. Determine if a transition plan "freeze" is required.
- Obtain a copy of the current organization chart indicating employees and open head count.
- Highlight, whenever possible, the essential managers and technical people that must be retained in the transition plan. This will be a combined judgment of the human resources department, the team members, and the functional management.
- Obtain summaries of all profit sharing, 401k, pension plans, and any incentives, bonuses, and commission plans in effect. Determine if any new or unusual plans have been implemented in recent months or are expected to be implemented within the next 12–18 months.
- Describe any stock, bonus, or option plans in effect including who is covered as well as the terms.
- Obtain summaries of all existing warrants, options, and commitments to employees. Determine if there is any buyout provision in any of the contracts. Determine if there are any golden parachutes in effect with any of the employees.
- Review existing union contracts to determine what impact, if any, change in stock ownership will have on the contract. Review the labor relations with shop stewards and union representatives to determine if they are reasonable. Each of these factors should be considered for all significant manufacturing or company operations on a worldwide basis. Consider using other parties to review these issues if you are not able to visit the facilities personally.
- Review turnover statistics to identify any critical areas. For example, if turnover is significant at one facility, there may be unusual problems that must be addressed before a successful integration.

- Assess the existing accrual status versus all employee benefit programs.

- Evaluate the target company management structure, considering your structure as well as the intended structure after the acquisition is completed. Determine the high-risk people and the impact on the acquisition if they leave the company. Consider developing incentives during the integration plan.

Regulatory Requirements

- Determine if there any significant registrations held by the company. These could be with the FDA, USDA, and the like. Also determine if an agency such as ISO 9000 has been reviewing the organization. Are registrations current and in effect?

- If a review by federal agencies or ISO agencies has occurred during the past 12–18 months, obtain copies of the reports. If there are significant deficiencies, these should be brought to the team leader's attention. If there are no significant deficiencies but only minor variances, determine how the company has addressed these. Does its operating procedure manuals provide reasonable guidelines for compliance with federal regulators?

- Are there reports by the EPA or environmental and safety agencies in foreign countries that have significant findings? These should be reviewed to determine if any serious financial exposures exist. Are reserves adequate for those exposures identified?

- Obtain representations from senior management at each location that they comply with regulations. Although overall legal representations will be made in the contract, it is best to hear from line management early in the negotiation process whether there are serious exposures. If they do arise, these can be considered in the contract negotiation and in the initial integration plan.

International Operations

- All international operations represent unusual business risks in an acquisition. The varying legal, social, and economic regulations and customs may significantly affect the cost of acquiring or integrating the target company. Either company personnel or contract personnel, such as local counsel or public accounting firms, should review all significant offshore operations. Generally, the same review questions as in the United States should be completed in the international environment. Regulations related to employees, contract agents, and distributors are of particular interest in the international environment. Many countries in Europe and Latin America have onerous provisions for employee or contract termination.

- Local counsel should be consulted about the potential acquisitions and integration plans. The international representatives should review consolidation plans.

Notes

1. "How Companies Can Marry Well," *Business Week* (March 4, 2002): 28.
2. Susan Willetts, "New HP Boasts of Contract Wins in the Months Ahead of Deal's Close," *Interactive Wall Street Journal* (May 7, 2002).
3. Pui-Wing Tam and Scott Thurm, "Hewlett-Packard, Compaq Present New Company, Sales Plans, Leaders," *Interactive Wall Street Journal* (May 8, 2002).
4. Susan Willetts, "New HP Boasts of Contract Wins in the Months Ahead of Deal's Close," *Interactive Wall Street Journal* (May 7, 2002).
5. Andy Serwer, "Michael Dell Rocks," *Fortune Magazine On-Line* (May 11, 1998).
6. Shawn Tully, "The Jamie Dimon Show," *Fortune Magazine* (July 22, 2002): 96.
7. John Koppisch, Gerry Kharmouch, and Kerry Capell, "It's Miller Time in Johannesburg," *Business Week* (April 22, 2002): 52.
8. "How Companies Can Marry Well," *Business Week* (March 4, 2002): 28.
9. Booz, Allen, and Hamilton, Inc., Consulting Firm, *Thought Leaders* (San Francisco: Jossey-Bass, 1998), 110.
10. Ronald N. Ashkenas, Lawrence J. DeMonaco, and Suzanne C. Francis, "Making the Deal Real: How GE Capital Integrates Acquisitions," *Harvard Business Review* (Jan.–Feb. 1998): 165.
11. "Chainsaw Al Goes to Camp Coleman," *Business Week* (March 16, 1998): 36.
12. Shawn Tully, "The Jamie Dimon Show," *Fortune Magazine* (July 22, 2002): 90.
13. Price Pritchett, Donald Robinson, Russell Clarkson, and Don Robinson, *After the Merger: The Authoritative Guide to Integration Success,* second edition (New York: McGraw-Hill, 1997), 118.
14. Molly Williams, "HP's Fiorina Takes on Hefty Job in Turning Around Merged Giant," *Interactive Wall Street Journal* (Sept. 5, 2001).

15. "HP Touts Cost Savings," *Silicon Valley/San Jose Business Journal* (Dec. 3, 2002).

16. "PC Sales Slowed Sharply in Second Period," *Interactive Wall Street Journal* (July 27, 1998).

17. Booz, Allen, and Hamilton, Inc., Consulting Firm, *Thought Leaders* (San Francisco: Jossey-Bass, 1998), 115.

18. "The New Massive Citigroup Puts Two Different Personalities at Top," *Interactive Wall Street Journal* (April 8, 2002).

19. Pui-Wing Tam and Scott Thurm, "Hewlett-Packard, Compaq Present New Company, Sales Plans, Leaders," *Interactive Wall Street Journal* (May 8, 2002).

20. Citicorp/Citibank press release, "Citicorp and Travelers Group to Merge, Creating Citigroup: The Global Leader in Financial Services" (April 6, 1998).

21. David Pringle, "New Chief in Europe Faces Challenge of Stitching Together HP, Compaq," *Interactive Wall Street Journal* (May 10, 2002).

22. Schedule 14D-1 under the Securities Exchange Act of 1934.

23. Molly Williams, "HP's Fiorina Takes on Hefty Job in Turning Around Merged Giant," *Interactive Wall Street Journal* (Sept. 5, 2001).

24. H. Unger, "The People Trauma of Major Mergers," *Journal of Industrial Management* (April 17, 1986): 10.

25. Pui-Wing Tam, "Carly Fiorina Manages Dual Roles with Organization, Commitment," *Interactive Wall Street Journal* (Feb. 7, 2002).

26. Pui-Wing Tam and Scott Thurm, "Hewlett-Packard, Compaq Present New Company, Sales Plans, Leaders," *Interactive Wall Street Journal* (May 8, 2002).

27. Shawn Tully, "Risky Business," *Fortune Magazine* (April 18, 2002): 116.

28. Sue Cartwright and Gary Cooper, *Managing Mergers, Acquisitions, and Strategic Alliances* (Oxford: Butterworth-Heinemann, 1997), 80.

29. Pui-Wing Tam, "HP Designs Workshops to Break Postmerger Ice," *Interactive Wall Street Journal* (July 11, 2002).

30. John A. Byrne and Ben Elgin, "The Cisco Hype," *Business Week* (Jan. 21, 2002): 60.

31. Gary McWilliams, "HP Leans Towards Its Managers in Setting Up New Organization," *Interactive Wall Street Journal* (May 6, 2002).

32. Nanette Byrnes and Julie Forster, "A Touch of Indigestion," *Business Week* (March 4, 2002): 66.

33. International patents often contain unusual restrictions, e.g., if a product has been used in commerce before application for an international patent, the patent may be denied. Careful research is essential.

34. "China's Crackdown on Smuggling Threatens Multinational's Sales," *Interactive Wall Street Journal* (Aug. 5, 1998).

Selected Bibliography

Booz, Allen, and Hamilton, Inc., Consulting Firm. *Thought Leaders*. San Francisco: Jossey-Bass. 1998.

Cartwright, Sue, and Gary Cooper. *Managing Mergers, Acquisitions, and Strategic Alliances*. Oxford: Butterworth-Heinemann. 1997.

Feldman, Mark L., and Michael F. Spratt. *Five Frogs on a Log: A CEO's Field Guide to Accelerating the Transition in Mergers, Acquisitions, and Gut Wrenching Change*. HarperCollins. 1998.

Haspeslagh, Philippe C., and David B. Jemison. *Managing Acquisitions*. New York: The Free Press. 1991.

Marks, Mitchell Lee, and Philip H. Mirvis. *Joining Forces: Making One Plus One Equal Three in Mergers, Acquisitions, and Alliances*. San Francisco: Jossey-Bass. 1998.

Pritchett, Price, Donald Robinson, Russell Clarkson, and Don Robinson. *After the Merger: The Authoritative Guide to Integration Success,* second edition. New York: McGraw-Hill. 1997.

Reed Lajoux, Alexandra. *The Art of M & A Integration: A Guide to Merging Resources, Processes and Responsibilities*. New York: McGraw-Hill. 1999.

Rock, Milton L., ed. *The Mergers and Acquisitions Handbook*. New York: McGraw-Hill. 1987, 1994.

Index

About the Author

MICHAEL P. GENDRON is a private investor and former Senior Vice President and Chief Financial Officer of Hill-Rom Inc., a global medical device company based in Batesville, Indiana.